AF291415

# 60 REMARKABLE ROOMS

### of the National Trust

# 60 REMARKABLE ROOMS

## of the National Trust

ELIZABETH GREEN, LUCY PORTEN AND JAMES ROTHWELL

INTRODUCTION BY MICHELLE OGUNDEHIN

*With entries by Frances Bailey, Sophie Chessum,
Mia Jackson and Katie Taylor*

National Trust

# Contents

SOUTH WEST
Drefsing Room
GROUND FLOOR
BLUE
DRESSING
ROOM.
LORD GREYS
ROOM.

# Introduction by Michelle Ogundehin

There are few things more evocative than stepping over the threshold of a historic home. One moment you are firmly in the present, the next you are held inside an atmosphere shaped by centuries. This is the magic of the National Trust. Its places do not merely preserve the past, they allow us to enter it. Rooms become time capsules, storytellers, stage sets left standing after the players have departed. And yet they are never still. They continue to breathe with meaning, because rooms, like people, hold memories long after events have passed.

For me, a lifelong devotee of interiors, a National Trust property has always been more than bricks and mortar. It is a portal. As a child I sensed this instinctively: the quiet thrill of stepping into a hall where crinolines once swished, the hush of a library lined with books whose spines had outlasted monarchs, the inexplicable feeling that you were being welcomed into someone else's world, even if that someone had been gone for aeons. As an adult, I understood that such responses were not imagined. Rooms tell tales – they always have. They speak of how people live, what they value, how they work, rest, entertain and dream.

This book presents 60 such rooms, chosen from the thousands cared for by the Trust. They are remarkable not just for their beauty or craftsmanship, but because each offers a window into a lived experience. Here, interiors become biography. They reflect the personalities, aspirations and preoccupations of the people who made them. Some are rooms of power, deliberately designed to impress. Others are rooms of purpose: retreats, built for solitude, comfort or contemplation. Many are spaces of labour, where invisible hands have left traces of their diligence. All are fragments of our collective story, told through timber and textiles, plaster and paint.

When I began working on this introduction, I expected simply to admire these spaces through a design lens. Instead, the project sent me down unexpected research paths. I found myself revisiting Oscar Wilde's 1882 lecture 'The House Beautiful', in which he argued that beauty

*Opposite* · Michelle Ogundehin (left) exploring Sissinghurst, Kent, with curator Lucy Porten, in October 2025.

*Frontispiece* · Detail of the interior of the Nostell Dolls' House, Nostell, West Yorkshire, which dates from around 1729–42 (NT 959710).

*Pages 4–5* · Servants' bells at Dunham Massey, Cheshire.

was not a luxury but a moral good, something capable of ennobling all those who encountered it. I was drawn again to John Ruskin's *The Seven Lamps of Architecture* (1849) – particularly the Lamp of Memory, his insistence that buildings carry the spirit of those who came before, and that to destroy them is to sever ourselves from our own history.

Both ideas feel woven into every room in this book. Wilde's belief in beauty as a civilising force is present in the quiet majesty of the Tithe Barn in Middle Littleton, the kinetic marvel of Heatherwick Studio's Glasshouse at Woolbeding, and even in a detail like the trio of brass taps in the Butler's Pantry at Castle Drogo. Ruskin's Lamp of Memory glows in Theodore Mander's Great Parlour at Wightwick Manor (opposite) – an extraordinary layering of personal passions, from William Morris prints to Japanese porcelain and Turkish rugs. But also, it flickers in the pomp of Lord Onslow's Marble Hall at Clandon Park, a vision that sadly neither he, nor his wife, nor the architect, ever lived to see completed.

As a design writer, TV presenter and homes therapist, I have spent decades exploring why rooms matter. As the former Editor-in-Chief of *ELLE Decoration*, I've seen more interiors than most people could visit in a lifetime – glossy, contemporary spaces crafted for magazines, architectural statements celebrated for innovation, homes meticulously arranged for contemporary

*Above left* · Oscar Wilde (1854–1900), author of 'The House Beautiful' (1882), in a photograph by Alfred Ellis from the collection at Smallhythe Place, Kent (NT 1122213).

*Above right* · John Ruskin (1819–1900), author of *The Seven Lamps of Architecture* (1849), in an Elliott & Fry carte-de-visite of 1867 at Lacock Abbey, Wiltshire (NT 1519580).

*Opposite* · The Great Parlour at Wightwick Manor, West Midlands.

life. But the rooms in this book offer something different. Some were created to project influence or sophistication, others were shaped quietly, by habit, necessity or personal preference. Whether lavish or modest, curated or accidental, each

*Above* • Vita Sackville-West's Tower Writing Room
at Sissinghurst, Kent.

room reflects the true conditions of the life it once held.

I must admit I have a favourite. I am always drawn to spaces with soul, where the air itself seems to carry memory. Nowhere was this more powerful than at Sissinghurst. Standing in Vita Sackville-West's Tower Writing Room (opposite), I felt her presence so keenly that the room seemed alive with her and her uncompromising devotion to beauty and words. However, after less than an hour, I felt like an interloper, compelled to return the sanctity of this most private of rooms back to her. That, to me, is the peculiar gift of a remarkable room: it can hold not just objects, but the lingering essence of a life.

This is why walking through a National Trust house can feel strangely intimate. You find yourself imagining the lives that unfolded in these spaces – the conversations, the arguments, the meals, the routines. You picture the hands that stitched the curtains, carved the balusters, swept the floors. And sometimes, unexpectedly, you feel seen. Because rooms contain universal experiences: childhood, work, rest, aspiration, ritual, love. They remind us that while times change, human needs do not.

In selecting these 60 interiors, the curators have created a journey through centuries of domestic, political, artistic and social history. They have included rooms that dazzle and rooms that soothe, rooms shaped by luxury and rooms shaped by necessity. They range from grand halls where visitors came to be impressed, to a modest Victorian terrace turned artwork that is just as astonishing. Together, they form a portrait not merely of architectural heritage, but of the lives that built this nation.

I hope, as you turn these pages, you feel the same sense of wonder that has accompanied me throughout my life whenever I enter a National Trust property. I hope you find yourself transported – not just into other eras, but into the lives of the people who made these rooms what they are. And I hope you come to see, as I have, that the spaces we inhabit are always far more than mere backdrops. They shape us. They tell our stories. And when preserved with care, they continue to speak – clearly, eloquently and with extraordinary humanity.

These rooms are remarkable. But more than that, they are reminders. That beauty matters. That memory endures. And that the way we shape our space shapes our lives.

Michelle Ogundehin

# The shape of our lives

Rooms are the human imagination made real and they resonate with histories that are both personal and universal. Birth, death and all the chapters of life in between are framed within rooms. We impress our taste and personality on them, fill them with meaningful and beautiful objects, and, in turn, they bear witness to the events both great and small that shape our lives.

*60 Remarkable Rooms of the National Trust* showcases the astonishingly rich array of interiors cared for by the Trust, from the opulence of Osterley's Neo-classical state rooms to the simple relatability of a Liverpool council-house parlour. The ways in which we respond to them are often deeply revealing about human nature – we are irresistibly inquisitive about the private spaces of others, we marvel at grandeur, and we are intrigued by rooms that have shaped and absorbed great moments in history.

Rooms are also the practical and artistic expressions of human occupation. They contain a wealth of evidence – the skill of the carpenter, plasterer, glazier and painter at work over the centuries, as well the hand of those who occu-

*Opposite* · Detail of the hallway at Mr Straw's House in Blyth Grove, Worksop, Nottinghamshire, an Edwardian semi largely unchanged since the 1930s.

pied these spaces. Many embody the creative vision of famous names – Grinling Gibbons, Louis Laguerre, Robert Adam, William Morris, Rex Whistler, Sibyl Colefax – while others bear the fingerprints and toolmarks of nameless builders and makers.

Perhaps most importantly, rooms can hold powerful emotional memories. They give shelter and comfort, and enable us to operate successfully as individuals, families and communities. We respond to rooms with all our senses – the deliciously tactile hand-polished boards of Loughwood's simple pine pews, the play of light and sound on the watery rill that trickles through Kedleston's Fishing Pavilion, a shaft of sunshine lancing through The Vyne Chapel's stained glass, the musty yet familiar scent of old tweed cloth wafting from Mr Straw's wardrobe, or the tang of ancient woodsmoke seeping from the walls of Chirk's Servants' Hall.

Rooms can transcend as well as enforce social barriers. Whether in a sumptuously draped, gilded bedchamber of state, as at Dunham Massey or Dyrham Park, or the spartan slope-ceilinged space at Birmingham's Back to Backs, the functional ingredient is the same – a bed in which to sleep, and to conduct the most intimate of human functions: birth, sex, death.

*Left* · The ground-floor passage at Red House, the home of William Morris in Bexleyheath, London. Morris designed it in 1859 in partnership with the architect Philip Webb in their signature Arts and Crafts style.

## Making the selection

The task of selecting just 60 from the thousands of spaces in the care of the National Trust proved to be a challenging but exciting one. Our principal aim is to delight and surprise you, our reader, with the range of rooms described in these pages. From the astonishing earthen dovecote in the derelict Tattershall Castle, to A la Ronde's fragile Shell Gallery, we hope that our selection will encourage you to visit and enjoy these truly remarkable rooms.

Some have been included for the history-makers who occupied them, such as the rural bedroom at Woolsthorpe Manor to which Sir Isaac Newton retreated from the plague, Chartwell's Dining Room, filled with the guests of the Churchills, or George Bernard Shaw's wonderful rotating Writing Shed.

From Chastleton's rugged, oak-pinnacled stairway to Florence Court's Rococo confection, many of the Trust's most intriguing spaces are those that interconnect grander rooms – corridors, lobbies and staircases. One of the oldest is the simple spiral stair at Old Soar Manor, dating from around 1290, and contrasting with magnificent staircase halls, such

*Below* · The Painted Staircase at Hanbury Hall, Worcestershire, with murals of around 1710 by Sir James Thornhill.

*Below* · The Grand Staircase at Petworth, West Sussex, with murals of 1718–20 by Louis Laguerre.

as Claydon's finely wrought Grand Staircase. The wealthiest homeowners sought out royally commissioned artists, resulting in the towering masterpieces of Louis Laguerre at Petworth, Gerard Lanscroon at Powis and Sir James Thornhill at Hanbury.

As well as some of the largest rooms, the selection also showcases what is usually the smallest, the loo. Mrs Greville's ritzy bathroom at Polesden Lacey is less typical perhaps than the Peckover privy with its peeling paint, or Llanerchaeron's multi-seated thunderboxes.

Places of worship have long provided pro-tection for those persecuted because of their faith as well as spaces to celebrate it. Staunton Harold's exquisitely decorated church was built as an act of defiance during the Commonwealth, and Moseley Old Hall's attic conceals a 17th-century chapel. Many priest holes survive, including at Coughton Court, home of the recusant Throckmorton family. Most moving of the Trust's chapel spaces is perhaps Stanley Spencer's Sandham Memorial Chapel, a shrine to the fallen of the First World War.

Now largely silent, former cathedrals of commerce and manufacturing survive in the slate landscape of north-west Wales and the cotton-milling counties of northern England.

*Right* • Stanley Spencer's decorative scheme for Sandham Memorial Chapel in Hampshire comprises 19 paintings.

But every village historically had its own hives of industry – cornmills, smithies and foundries. At Finch Foundry, on the fringes of Dartmoor, the plash of the waterwheel, the clang of hammer on anvil and the metallic smokiness of the furnace make this space a sensory and nostalgic feast.

In addition to the high-profile historic places that it cares for, the Trust also looks after cottages, houses and farms available across the wider estate for tenants to let. The majority of rooms in the care of the National Trust are therefore still in everyday use as homes and places of work. Mostly rural, these cottages, barns and field shelters – numbering in the thousands – play a vital part in our nation's food production and encourage a flourishing natural environment. By necessity, the rooms included here are those that are accessible to visitors or available for rental as holiday cottages.

## The evolution of the room

The chronological development of architecture, as represented within the National Trust, is explored in *60 Remarkable Buildings*, the companion volume to this book.

The relationship between the design of the whole building in its wider setting and the spaces within it is one that changes with the centuries, often inflected by local materials, shifting tastes and fashions, or the demands of etiquette and social customs.

*Above* · The Priest's Hole in the Tower Room at Coughton Court, Warwickshire, viewed from above.

*Opposite* · A full-length Spinning Mule at Quarry Bank Mill in Cheshire, an 18th-century textile mill that continues to produce fabric on its historic Lancashire looms.

Our earliest rooms are often simple in design. Their form is purely functional and governed by the limitations of local materials and skills – for example, Cymryd Isaf's sleeping loft and Tintagel's Hall. The hall house of the Middle Ages was so-called because the principal space was a multi-functional hall. Walls were limewashed and furniture sparse and simple. Windows, often unglazed, were inserted only where required for light or ventilation and little consideration was given to elevational design. However, the glory of medieval architecture is the celebration of the carpenter's skill and demonstration of wealth seen in the great roofs and screens of the period. The interlaced wind braces of Cotehele's hall roof, or the quatrefoiled panelling at Rufford Old Hall richly demonstrate the combination of structural heft and fine ornament.

Later, the Elizabethan age saw advances in the manufacture of glass coincide with the arrival of Renaissance architectural influences. Internal planning reduced the hall to an entry and circulation space. Views in and out of rooms were prized, and the appearance of elevations became as important as the internal arrangement and decoration of space, as seen at Hardwick and Little Moreton Hall.

The chronology of rooms reveals an inevitable bulge in the 18th century. The fascination with the Classical world that animates the designs of Robert Adam, James Wyatt, James Paine and their contemporaries is widely found in the grand rooms of places such as Croome, Berrington and Castle Coole. The geometrical motifs and heroic swags of Classical Greece and Italy reworked into plaster ceilings and whole rooms that could have been lifted from Pompeii are executed exquisitely, as by Robert Adam in Osterley's Etruscan Dressing Room.

The Victorians found fascination in antiquarianism, and architecture and design became focussed on stylistic revivals. Most prominent was the Gothic Revival, writ large in National Trust rooms, such as Pugin's Cromwell Hall at Chirk Castle and the extraordinary chapel at Tyntesfield, where Arthur Blomfield invoked the flourish of French Gothic to elevate a space for family worship into la Sainte-Chapelle in miniature. 19th-century mechanisation and mass production changed the way in which people set about furnishing their rooms. Style could be purchased, ready-made, in goods ranging from wallpapers and fabrics to ceramics and furniture. The Arts and Crafts Movement, spearheaded by deep thinkers and idealists, such as William Morris, arose in ideological opposition to this. The Great Exhibition of 1851, housed in Joseph Paxton's Crystal Palace, showcased the great scientific innovations and industrial triumphs of the age, alongside handmade treasures from around the world, exemplifying both modern-day advances and traditional craft skills.

At Cragside, William, 1st Lord Armstrong, embraced these emerging technologies and installed the world's first hydro-electric power system with a control room for the Keeper of the Electric Light. Harnessing Northumberland's generous rainfall, the electricity generated was initially used to power an arc lamp in the picture gallery in 1878. The advent of electric light would transform our experience of interior spaces.

Between and after the two world wars, interior design increasingly turned away from the reimagining of past glories to explore new directions. Stellar spaces by Ernő Goldfinger at Willow Road and Patrick Gwynne at The Homewood rub their skinny minimalist shoulders with the softer, otherworldly style of Rex Whistler at Mottisfont and Plas Newydd.

Most recently, National Trust commissions at Woolbeding and Runnymede, Heatherwick Studio's spiky fingers pointing heavenwards contrasting with the reflective pool of Mark Wallinger and Studio Octopi's *Writ in Water*, point to the future, where the definition of 'room' becomes blurred, the boundary between interior and exterior rendered uncertain.

*Right* · The previous classical Georgian interior of the Cromwell Hall at Chirk Castle, Wrexham, was given a Gothic Revival makeover by A.W.N. Pugin in 1845.

## International connections

The lure of global culture has influenced interior design for centuries. From the early 17th century and the rise of the East India Trading Company, hand-painted papers were imported from China, bringing the unattainable landscapes of East Asia to the wealthy homes of Europe. South-Asian ivory, lacquered furniture and Chinese and Japanese ceramics became hugely fashionable, inspiring British makers to adopt their styles. Erddig's state bedroom, with its Chinese silk hangings, lacquered cabinets and hand-painted wallpaper is an excellent example among many.

However, there are human costs attached to the desire for fine materials. The growing trade in Central American and West Indian mahogany for furniture from the 17th century onwards was entwined with the transatlantic trade in enslaved African people. Jamaican mahogany was felled to create sugar plantations and the resulting boom in the fine furniture industry is widely visible in country house interiors, from mahogany panelling to the furniture of makers such as Thomas Chippendale.

The desire to capture and mimic what is 'exotic' and foreign has seen whole rooms uprooted from their original locations, whether a transient

*Right* • The first-floor Living Room at The Homewood, the Modernist house that Patrick Gwynne designed and built for his parents in Esher, Surrey, in the late 1930s.

space, such as Tīpū Sultān's tent at Powis Castle, or Waddesdon's Green Boudoir (in fact, a Parisian *salon*), transplanted whole, in a phenomenon widely seen in the Gilded Age 'palaces' of fashionable American Society.

The galleries of great international museums, such as the New York Met or the V&A in London, now hold some of the finest interiors that once graced great European houses. Croome Park's exquisite Robert Adam Tapestry Room is across the Atlantic in The Met's British Galleries, but happily its near twin can be seen, still in situ, at Osterley Park. Falling on hard times in the 1890s, the Strickland family of Sizergh Castle sold the panelling, bed and stained glass of the Inlaid Chamber to the V&A. Thankfully, in 1999, the National Trust restored it to its historic home.

**Protecting the past, eyeing the future**

Since the mid-1950s, listing and other heritage designations have increasingly helped to protect places of historical significance. However, the moveable nature of furnishing, the fragility of decorated surfaces, and the intangible qualities of social and sensory history associated with our rooms can make them harder to protect.

The Country Houses Act of 1937 enabled the National Trust to take into its care whole historic houses and their collections, preserving interiors for future generations. Today, we can stroll through rooms hung with astonishing art collections, hand-crafted furniture and textiles that have endured over the centuries.

Climate change, government policy, economic fluctuation and many other factors impact on our ability as a society to care for our heritage. Climate change, for example, has brought higher rainfall, leading to flooding in historic buildings, while rising temperatures have led to a proliferation of pests that threaten fragile textiles. However, creative solutions are being found, such as at Blickling, where a tiny wasp has been deployed as a natural predator to curb the spread of the clothes moth.

These complex challenges demand urgent strategic responses if we are to safeguard these extraordinary survivors so that future generations of visitors can be as astonished and intrigued by them as we are today.

We hope that you enjoy our selection of remarkable rooms, and that you find yourself inspired to explore further and perhaps even become involved in protecting a historic place that is special to you.

Elizabeth Green, Lucy Porten
and James Rothwell

*Opposite* · The Kitchen at 20 Forthlin Road, Liverpool, the childhood home of Sir Paul McCartney.

*Overleaf* · The Bathroom at Clouds Hill, the Dorset retreat of T.E. Lawrence, better known as 'Lawrence of Arabia'.

# 60
# REMARKABLE
# ROOMS

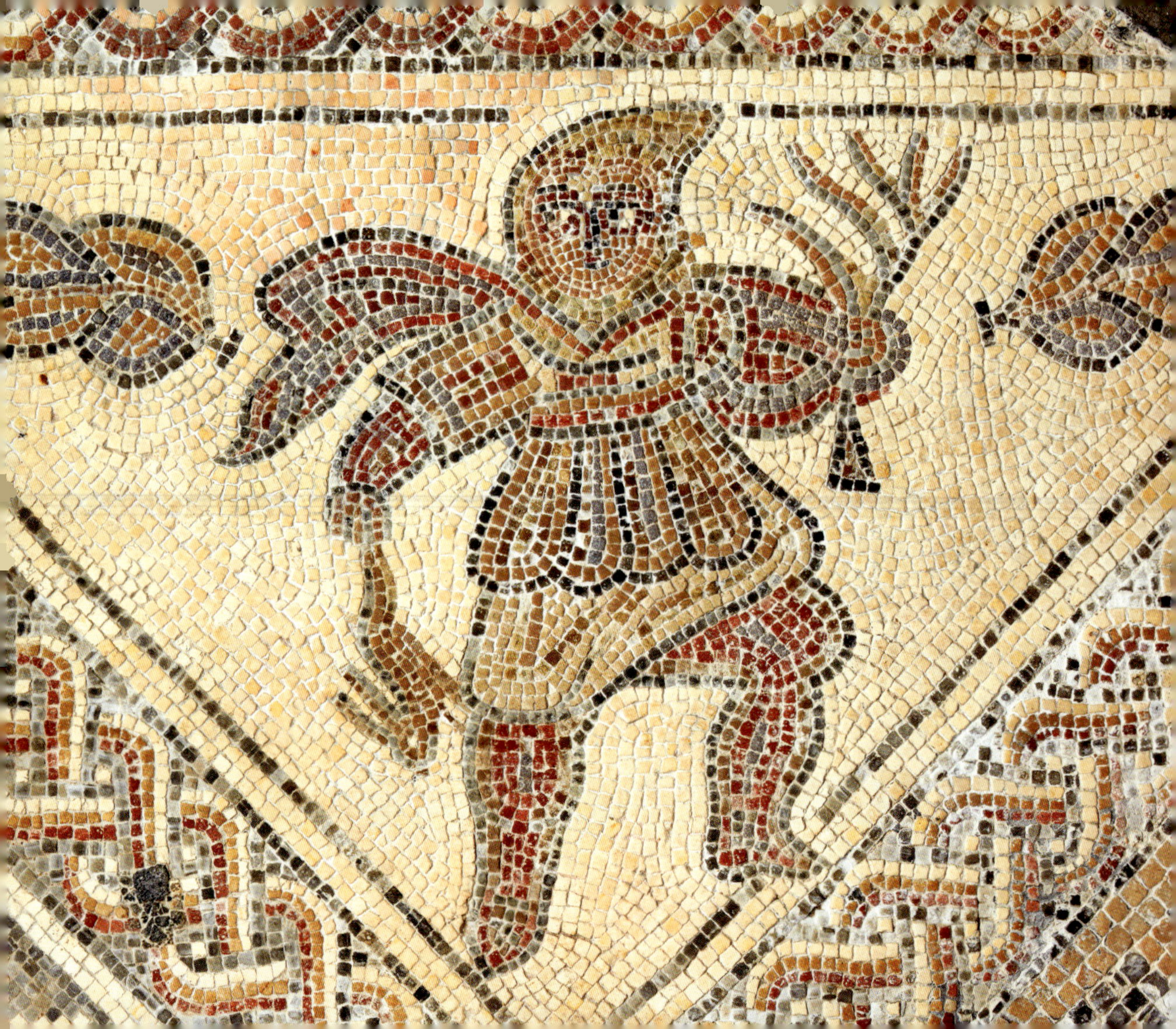

# Competitive consumption

Surrounded by highly productive farmland, Chedworth Roman Villa was part of a network of landed estates associated with Corinium, modern-day Cirencester, the capital of Roman Britain. The Grand Dining Room, or *triclinium*, was the finest room in this impressive villa.

It was a ritualistic, controlled social space, dedicated to competitive consumption. Richly decorated and complete with a hypocaust, it was comfortable and well-heated.

Following the ritual of bathing (*tepidarium*, *caldarium* and *frigidarium*), guests would have been anointed with fragrant oils before moving through to the lobby to be welcomed and prepared to dine 'among the Gods'.

The magnificent mosaic floor comprises two intricate and vibrant designs. The first consists of a square filled with geometric key patterns and interlaced knotwork in red, ochre, white and black. Either side of this central 'carpet', a panel of foliage pours forth from an urn. Next comes a cabled border, and the whole is bounded within a course of red and white chevron patterns and a plaited rope. Although damaged, the second, octagonal portion is even more remarkable. Each field holds a scene depicting Bacchus and Ariadne. Corner triangles are peopled with representations of the seasons (the figure opposite is Winter). The *tesserae* are all cut from local stone, except for the red tiles, which are tiny baked-earth bricks.

It is easy to see here, in Chedworth's intricate and formal beauty, the forerunner of the finely woven Neo-classical carpets that adorn many a modern mansion floor. EG

**Chedworth Roman Villa, Gloucestershire** • Grand Dining Room • *4th century* • *Bought by public subscription, 1924*

*Left* • The surviving mosaic floor of Chedworth's Grand Dining Room in a drawing by Luigi Thompson.

# Gothic glamour

There is a dash of 1930s Hollywood about the Dining Room at Anglesey Abbey. With its vaulted ceiling springing dramatically from octagonal Alwalton marble columns, great hooded chimneypiece, iron chandelier and ornate 16th- and 17th-century dark wood furniture, Errol Flynn would not look entirely out of place sprawling nonchalantly at the head of the long refectory table at its centre. This dramatic space is not, however, a 20th-century conceit but a rare example of a largely intact monastic space from the mid-13th century.

A hospital was founded at Anglesey in Cambridgeshire, probably by Henry I in 1135, and this was converted into a priory of Augustinian canons by a Master Lawrence, who died in 1236. Almost the entire complex, including a church, had been completed by then at his personal expense and it is highly likely that this included the Dining Room, which was probably built as a calefactory, or warming room, for the monks. Though fragments of the priory buildings survive throughout the principal ranges of the house, it is only here that medieval work is obvious, and it is little short of a miracle that this complete space has survived. It withstood the plunder of the rest of the complex by the first secular owner and was retained as part of

the service rooms of the smart gabled house
built on the site in the Jacobean period. In the
19th century, with the Gothic back in vogue, its
fortunes rose and it became the entrance hall
of the newly dubbed Anglesey Abbey.

When the American-born 1st Lord Fairhaven
(1896–1966) remodelled and extended the house
between the wars, his new Dining Room became
the focus for entertaining guests, including
members of the royal family. He introduced
the chimneypiece, seemingly late medieval but
actually modern and made of composite stone,
and he selected suitably ancient furniture,
including a richly carved German oak cabinet
dated 1509. Among the other treasures with
which he bedecked the room is a 16th-century
bronze salamander, the symbol of François I,
King of France (1494–1547), and the antique-
inspired *Shield of Achilles*, designed by John
Flaxman (1755–1826), the jewel of the house's
silver collection. JR

**Anglesey Abbey, Cambridgeshire** · Dining Room · *1236
and 1930s* · *Bequeathed by the 1st Lord Fairhaven, 1966*

*Opposite* · *Shield of Achilles*, Philip Rundell, designed
by John Flaxman, depicting Apollo surrounded by the
constellations, silver-gilt, 1822/3 (NT 516395).

*Right* · Detail of the intricate early 16th-century German
oak cabinet in the Dining Room at Anglesey Abbey,
Cambridgeshire (NT 514380).

# Tax haven

Shafts of sunlight piercing the gloom bring the interior of Middle Littleton Tithe Barn to life. Built soon after 1315 for Evesham Abbey, this cavernous space would once have been filled with grain, levied as a tax on the local population. The 'tithe' – a tenth of the harvest – was originally paid in corn, but it is likely that this barn held a variety of produce, including oats, wheat and barley.

A vital source of food for the Abbot and his charges, grains were also used for brewing, and as food for the animals that tilled the land and provided hides for clothing and as vellum for manuscripts. The magnificent barn would have been part of a substantial farming complex, a secure vault protecting the riches within.

The cool interior is softly aired by deeply splayed ventilation slits, keeping mould and rot at bay, while the soaring roof sheltered its precious contents from the weather. Its walls and floor are built of Blue Lias stone with Cotswold stone dressings and stone tile roof. This vast room is 42 metres long, 9 metres wide and 12 metres high, made up of eleven bays, articulated by huge oak raised crucks and, at either end, aisle trusses. The porches, of which there were originally four, gave access for carts and provided a breezy threshing floor, whose stones are now cracked and polished with age. EG

**Middle Littleton, Worcestershire** · Tithe barn ·
*After 1315 · Given by Mr and Mrs J.W. Keyte, 1975*

# Narrow escape

The passion for all things Arthurian in the 19th century nearly did for what is now the oldest structure on Tintagel's principal street. As neat boarding houses sprang up to accommodate visitors to the nearby castle – according to legend, the location of King Arthur's conception – the wrecking ball drew ever closer. This low-lying building, armadillo-like to withstand Atlantic gales and intensely charming with its wave-like roof, was offered for redevelopment but saved in 1895 by a local artist, Catherine Johns.

As built in the late 14th century, the house consisted of three rooms, dominated by the Hall at its centre, which must originally have been heated by an open hearth. The smoke would have permeated through the exposed roof structure above, gradually blackening the timbers, which stand in stark contrast to the neatly whitewashed walls. In the early 17th century the room gained the luxury of a chimneystack, upgraded in the 19th century by the addition of a particular feature of Devon and Cornwall, the cloam, or clay, bread oven (akin to a pizza oven), which is still functional today. The house served briefly as a letter-receiving office in the 1870s, during which time letters appear to have been posted through a slot in the Hall's principal window. JR

**Tintagel Old Post Office, Cornwall** · Hall · *Late 14th century and early 17th century · Purchased, 1903*

INRI

# Fit for a king

Henry VIII (1491–1547) and Anne Boleyn (*c.*1500–36) would have worshipped in this Chapel while staying at The Vyne in October 1535, just months before the queen's downfall and execution. They would have looked down from special closets at an upper level, one of which survives almost intact with a striped decorative scheme intended to evoke fashionable textile hangings.

The Chapel, of a magnificence not recorded outside the royal palaces of Tudor England, was constructed for the king's Lord Chamberlain, William, 1st Lord Sandys (*c.*1470–1540), and it reflects his importance as a patron of the finest craftsmen from England and continental Europe. The spectacular and richly coloured stained glass in the east windows, which contains scenes from the life of Christ as well as royal portraits, was created by a team of glaziers from the Low Countries, recruited by Sandys himself while in Calais in 1522. The carved oak stalls rival those in royal chapels such as St George's, Windsor, and the tiles were made in Flanders to Italian designs. JR

**The Vyne, Hampshire** · Chapel · *Early 16th century* · *Bequeathed by Sir Charles Chute, Bt, 1956*

# War and peace

Cotehele was built by the Edgcumbe family as a symbol of their power and great wealth but also to accommodate a large household. To that end Sir Piers Edgcumbe (1468/9–1539), who fought against the French under Henry VIII (1491–1547), completed the romantic stone building by erecting a new great hall. In it his servants and retainers could dine on a daily basis, and at times of feasts he and his family would have joined them, seated on a table at the 'high' end, which would originally have had an elevated dais. A great, granite-framed window demarcates the importance of this part of the room, as does the massive Tudor-arched fireplace opposite. Crowning the entire space is a spectacular roof, which, with its elaborately moulded timbers, is both a practical solution to covering a large expanse and a piece of showmanship.

Great halls were often repositories for arms and armour – ready for use in times of trouble, and a symbol of power and strength when the country was at peace. Among the collection still displayed on the walls at Cotehele are pieces that could have been deployed by Sir Piers, although many were only brought together here in the 18th and 19th centuries. As well as examples from England there are numerous important representations from Asia and Africa.

Also harking back to ancient traditions and practices is the Cotehele garland, an extraordinary assemblage of tens of thousands of dried flowers and foliage swagged across the entire length of the hall at Christmas. In the Tudor period festive entertainments and feasting, known as junketing, might well have been put on for the people of the locality at the expense of the lord of the manor, and the Great Hall would have been suitably bedecked for the occasion. JR

**Cotehele, Cornwall** · Great Hall · *c.1520* · *National Land Fund, 1947*

# Treasures of the tower

The mid-16th century in England saw a surge of interest in the Classical design language of continental Europe. Nowhere is this more powerfully represented than at Lacock Abbey, where Sir William Sharington (*c.*1495–1553) constructed an octagonal three-storey tower. He was creating a Renaissance country house out of the abbey buildings, which had been acquired following dissolution. The central floor of the protruding tower was to provide a strong room in which he could secure and admire precious objects.

A massive iron door gives access to the cool, stoney interior, the pendants of its rib vault bearing Sharington's scorpion emblem and its deeply recessed windows restricted in size to keep out intruders. Treasures and important documents could be taken from the bracketed shelves and recesses for inspection at the central, octagonal table. With its marble top supported by four leering satyrs, this is a precious treasure in itself and one that is exceptional for having survived in the position for which it was created nearly 500 years ago. JR

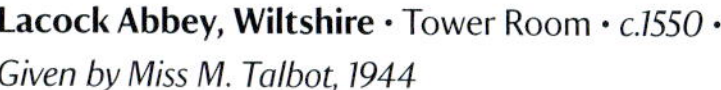

**Lacock Abbey, Wiltshire** · Tower Room · *c.1550* · *Given by Miss M. Talbot, 1944*

# Home improvement

The hamlet of 'Kymrid' is first mentioned in the *Record of Caernarfon* in 1352 as a group of *gafaelion*, or parcels of land, in the Dyffryn Conwy township of Castell. However, this house dates from a little later. Probably replacing a temporary structure, Cymryd Isaf's medieval hall was constructed from timbers that, according to dendrochronology, were felled around 1500.

The builders of Cymryd Isaf were out to impress. They paid their carpenter well to carve soft scalloping, or cusping, to the two oak struts at the apex of their great hall roof. Its gnarly oak skeleton is blackened by smoke from the fire that once burned on a stone hearth in the centre of the hall floor.

However, the sleeping loft only came into being during the mid-16th century, when the owners divided the open hall, inserting a first floor and replacing the central hearth with a lateral fireplace in a bout of home improvement.

Initially, only the end bay was converted, with a ladder leading up from the pantry below. You can still see fragments of the wattle and daub and panelled partition that divided the pantry loft from the open hall. Successive generations extended the loft, tucking in between tie beams and rafters, eventually creating a three-bay sleeping loft, with dormers to bring light, and a huge, solid-oak-tread staircase giving access from the hall below. EG

**Cymryd Isaf, Conwy** · Sleeping loft · *Mid-16th century* · *Given by Miss D. Glynne, 2007*

# Tudor tour de force

There is something distinctly nautical about the Long Gallery at Little Moreton Hall. Its uninterrupted 16th-century glazing is reminiscent of the uppermost part of the stern of a great galleon, and the floor undulates as if a wave is running its full length. The precariously perched exterior, meanwhile, seems to have landed on the roof below and has been aptly described as resembling 'a stranded Noah's Ark'.

The Moretons of Little Moreton were on the rise in the 16th century, and it was William Moreton II (*c.*1510–63) who, towards the end of his life, commenced the house's south range. The gallery that so dramatically crowns it is a tour de force of Tudor craftsmanship, the highly skilled carpentry work being carried out 'according to the devyse thereof devised twixt me [William Moreton] and Richard Dale [carpenter]'. Arch-braced roof trusses allowed for greater headroom and for a visually light construction but were insufficient for the weight of the gritstone roof; hence the reinforcing cross-beams and the uneven structural settling that adds so much to the charm of the space. Plasterwork at either end of the gallery pronounces sober Protestant ethics, but fun was evidently permitted too, early 17th-century tennis balls having been recovered from behind the panelling. JR

**Little Moreton Hall, Cheshire** · Long Gallery · *1560s* ·
*Given by Bishop Abraham and Mr R. Abraham, 1938*

# The room that roamed

It is rare for a room to travel the length of the country – and even rarer for it to come back again, but that is what happened to Sizergh's Inlaid Chamber. In 1891 the cash-strapped Walter Charles Strickland (1825–1903) sold the panelling to the Victoria and Albert Museum, London, adding the bed and stained glass five years later for a combined total of £1,400 (the equivalent of around £150,000 today). Just over a century later, in 1999, the opportunity arose to reinstate the room and now it is hard to believe it has ever been away.

This sumptuous state bedchamber was fitted up around 1580, high up in the tower that dominates this ancient Lakeland house. There is an impressive plaster ceiling, richly decorated and textured, but it is the inlaid oak panelling that makes this room truly exceptional. It is considered the finest ever made for an English country house, the inlays of light poplar and black bog-oak creating intricate geometrical and foliate scrolling patterns within an architectural framework of the highest sophistication. JR

**Sizergh, Cumbria** · Inlaid Chamber · *c.1580* · *Given by Mr and the Hon. Mrs H. Hornyold-Strickland and Lt-Cdr T. Hornyold-Strickland, 1950*

# Dazzling decor

Hardwick Hall is a potent statement of female power in the Elizabethan age, and Elizabeth Hardwick, Countess of Shrewsbury (*c.*1521–1608), popularly known as Bess of Hardwick, was one of the most powerful women of the time.

Bess's architect, Robert Smythson, drew upon Italian Renaissance architecture in his treatment of elevations and the arrangement of interior spaces. The *piano nobile* is located on the second floor and reaching it is a carefully choreographed experience. The Grand Stair emerges onto a brightly lit landing, facing the imposing doorway into the High Great Chamber, resplendent with Bess's coat of arms.

While today its colours seem muted, this room once dazzled; expensive pigments suffusing paint and cloth, some interwoven with metal threads, glinting in shafts of sunlight from the heavily glazed west wall. The woodland hunting scenes of the towering frieze are vividly animated, and the royal coat of arms is proudly picked out in red, blue and gold above the cool Neoclassical alabaster of the fireplace. Beneath this, eight 'peeces of fayre tapestrie hangings of the stories of Ulisses eleven foote deepe' (see page 53) and carved wainscotting are described in a 1601 inventory.

Today, the impact of the room is principally in the grandeur of the architecture. In 1601, however, it was sumptuously furnished with all that Bess required for her comfort: tables draped with Turkey carpets; a carved and gilded cupboard; silk-upholstered chairs with gold fringes; and a host of stools in kaleidoscopic velvets, two of them set with marble decoration.

One of the few items of furniture still in situ is the eglantine table. Created around 1570, it has an intricately inlaid top of walnut, fruitwood and limewood marquetry depicting musical instruments and scores, playing cards, gaming boards and strapwork, with the motto 'The redolent smell of Eglantine (sweet briar rose), We stags exalt to the Divine'.

Portraits including King Henry VIII, Queen Elizabeth, Queen Mary, Edward VI and Cardinal Wolsey hung alongside pictures of 'the fowre partes of the worlde'. Finally, bringing an additional flourish to an exceptional room, were a looking glass 'paynted about with the Armes of England', and brass andirons.

By day, Bess's High Great Chamber still astonishes, but by night it must have seemed magical, with every silver fringe and gilded frame shimmering in the light of a thousand candles. EG

**Hardwick Hall, Derbyshire** · High Great Chamber · *Robert Smythson (c.1535–1614)* · *1590s* · *National Land Fund, 1959*

# Ironclad evidence

In the early 17th century Richard Braithwaite recommended that a great landowner 'ought to have more care for the safe keeping of his Evidence, than either of his plate [silver and gold] or Jewells'. Evidence in this context meant legal and other documents relating to his or her lands – title deeds, wills, marriage settlements, leases, accounts of receipts and payments – but also proof of ancestry, patents of nobility and correspondence.

No one took this more seriously than Elizabeth Hardwick, Countess of Shrewsbury (*c.*1521–1608), popularly known as Bess of Hardwick, who has been described by Mark Girouard as, among other things, 'a businesswoman, a money maker, a land-amasser, a builder of houses, an indefatigable collector of the trappings of wealth and power, and inordinately ambitious, both for herself and her children'. All of that produced a great deal of 'Evidence' and when she constructed the New Hall at Hardwick in the 1590s, a suitable room, known as an evidence house, had to be incorporated.

Protection from fire and theft was essential and thus the space has a masonry vault, thick walls, a single small window fitted with interlocking iron bars and a heavily bolted door to which, for good measure, additional metal sheets were fitted in 1603. To contain the precious documents, a total of 492 oak drawers or boxes were fitted around the walls, raised off the floor to avoid damp, and provided with a ladder to reach the upper tiers. Numbers were painted on the front of each box, the sequence commencing from above the entrance door and proceeding in horizontal tiers, ending in the bottom corner to the right of the window. Silk tassels served as drawer-pulls and some miraculously survive, although many have been replaced with more robust wooden knobs. JR

**Hardwick Hall, Derbyshire** · Evidence House · *Robert Smythson (c.1535–1614)* · *1590s* · *National Land Fund, 1959*

# Masterly treatment

Thomas Sackville, 1st Earl of Dorset (c.1536–1608), was second cousin to Queen Elizabeth I (1533–1603) and an immensely successful and wealthy courtier. He served as Lord High Treasurer to the queen and later to King James I (1566–1625), retaining the role until his death, which occurred while he was seated at the Privy Council table. Having decided late in life to make Knole in Kent his principal residence, he set about adapting the colossal medieval and 16th-century building. He intended it to express his elevated status, wealth and taste, as well as to allow the hosting of that much sought-after event – the visit of a sovereign. Critical to this was the provision of a state apartment, which consisted of a great chamber (now the Ballroom), withdrawing chamber (the Reynolds Room), gallery (the Cartoon Gallery) and bedchamber (the King's Room).

A gallery such as this was for communication – here leading from the withdrawing chamber to the bedchamber – but also for recreation and display. It needed to be worthy of a royal visitor and its high status required embellishment by the finest craftspeople. Richard Dungan (d.1609), Master Plasterer to the king, was responsible for the ceiling, with its flowing pattern of serpentine ribs interspersed with

botanical emblems, while the sumptuous marble chimneypiece may be by the king's Master Mason, Cornelius Cure (d.*c*.1608). Further rich treatment can be seen on the pilasters of the window wall, which are carved with grotesques including arms and armour, birds, monkeys and garlands of fruit and flowers, all fictively suspended from rams' heads.

Tudor and Jacobean galleries were often hung with historical portraits and the 1st Earl followed that trend, displaying the likenesses of English worthies as well as foreign military leaders against whom England had fought. Lord Dorset included a portrait of himself and was thus presented as a key figure in the nation's history. The paintings were relocated to the nearby Brown Gallery in the early 18th century to make way for six copies of Raphael's famous portrayal of scenes from the lives of saints Paul and Peter. The originals, now in the Victoria and Albert Museum, London, were produced as cartoons, or designs from which tapestries could be woven, and thus the name of this room changed from the Matted Gallery, after the rush matting on the floor, to the Cartoon Gallery, after the paintings – or cartoons – on the wall. JR

**Knole, Kent** · Cartoon Gallery · *1605–8* · *Given by the 4th Lord Sackville, 1946*

*Left* · Detail of *The Healing of the Lame Man* (after Raphael), one of a set of six copies of Raphael's cartoons in the Cartoon Gallery, Knole, Kent (NT 129945).

# Stairway to heaven

Jacobean architects were faced with the challenge of combining fashionable external symmetry with stubbornly asymmetrical house plans. At Chastleton this necessitated a pair of staircases to reach the upper floors from either end of the double-height Great Hall. The stairs are set back from the main façade in matching battlemented towers but inside they express their different purposes.

The oak East Staircase, which started at ground floor level and was built around an open core, led from the upper end of the Great Hall and was intended only for the most important guests. It was reconstructed in the 19th century. The West Staircase, however, which would have seen heavy use by servants and family, survives largely intact. Ascending from the kitchens in the basement to the second floor Long Gallery, it is simply detailed with an old-fashioned rising newel and an enclosed core. At the top, Jacobean balusters and pierced obelisk finials are set around a square enclosure known as a pulpit. JR

**Chastleton House, Oxfordshire** · West Staircase · *c.1610 · National Heritage Memorial Fund, 1991*

# Miniature gallery

The Green Closet at Ham House is a jewel-like rarity – a survivor. No other cabinet room from the 17th century has endured as well, with so many of its contents, its collection of paintings and miniatures so exceptional in both their size and setting. Sadly, the closets of Charles I, which inspired and influenced this room, are now lost.

The most private room in the houses of the elite, including those of the Crown, was a closet. Small, intimate and often richly decorated, only those closest to the monarch or house owner would be granted entry. Most adjoined a bedchamber but in the case of the Green Closet it was, originally, only accessible through a door off the Long Gallery. This suggests its use as a *studiolo* or art closet, a cabinet room where smaller artworks, miniatures, treasures and rarities might be displayed, admired and studied (not least as larger paintings could be viewed in the adjoining Gallery). It was a precious space guarded by handsome brass and steel locks and bolts, still operated with the original key today.

Ham House was built by Sir Thomas Vavasour (1560–1620), soldier, courtier and Knight Marshal to James I, in 1610. The Green Closet was created by William Murray (c.1600–55), who leased the estate from 1626 and was later made

1st Earl of Dysart. Murray had been a page to Prince Charles, joining his lessons and growing up alongside him. Later, when the prince became King Charles I (1600–49), Murray was appointed Groom of the Bedchamber and travelled abroad with the king.

The room originally had one door and two windows, but now has two doors and one window. The present window, originally longer, faces north towards the River Thames. North light, often more diffused, constant and cooler, was considered beneficial to gallery spaces, allowing artworks to be seen at their best and avoiding harsh sunlight and shadows.

An inventory of 1655 describes the room as having 'hanginges of greene stuffe', with a couch, chair and two stools 'of the same stuffe'. 'Stuff' was a general term used to describe all manner of fabrics but it seems likely to mean a silk damask here. Above the chimneypiece a painted scene, thought to depict Jupiter and Antiope, includes a draped green canopy of the same colour. The coving elsewhere is filled with images of playful nymphs, satyrs and putti. These are in tempera on paper and are based on designs by Polidoro da Caravaggio (c.1495–1543) – the originals works, acquired by Charles I in 1637, remain in the Royal Collection. They surround an image, on the ceiling, of *Flora with Cupids and Clouds* (opposite).

We cannot be sure of the exact picture hang in William Murray's time but the inventories of the 1670s and 1680s list the number of pictures to be in the fifties. The room survived largely intact into the age of photography and images of 1904 and *c.*1920 show a rich, dense display not unlike that of today. LP

**Ham House, Surrey** · Green Closet · *William Murray (c.1600–55)* · *1637–9* · *Given by Sir Lyonel Tollemache and Mr C.L.N. Tollemache, 1948*

# Humble house of worship

Being a nonconformist worshipper in the mid-17th century was a risky business. The congregation of Loughwood's Baptist Meeting House were known to travel great distances to worship at this discreet little building, tucked into the hillside beneath a thatched roof, looking more like a cottage than a church. Going against the doctrine of the Church of England could lead to imprisonment, transportation, or even death, and guards were stationed at the meeting house door during services to keep watch for the approach of law-enforcing soldiers. It was only following the Act of Toleration in 1688 that people were able to openly follow nonconformist beliefs.

The earliest record of a Baptist church at Loughwood is in 1653, and a document from 1657 details activities, including prayer, discussion and the breaking of bread, beginning at 7am, and running throughout the day. Food was prepared and shared, a room within the meeting house had a fire to warm chilled travellers, and there was a stable in the graveyard for horses to rest. This was clearly a close and devoted community.

A simple interior of tapering limewashed walls beneath a plain barrel vault is lit by splayed square openings with round-headed and leaded

windows. The floor of the central aisle has a beaten lime-ash surface with a later brick finish to the warming room at the rear. The fittings inside the meeting house – including a now wheezy harmonium – mostly date to more recent times. However, the gallery is of an early date, panelled with a deep moulded frieze and base, and pilasters supporting book or music stands. The importance of the gallery is emphasised by dark staining, to match the pulpit it faces. The pulpit is octagonal and is raised up above the 'Big Seat', beneath which is a full-immersion baptismal font. The pale polished pine box pews are 19th century, and a handsome clock, made by John Tratt of Colyton, presides over proceedings.

The Reverend Isaac Hann, 'An old Disciple', is beautifully commemorated in a handsome slate tablet on the north wall: *Wit sparkled in his pleasing Face / With Zeal his Heart was fir'd / Few Ministers so humble were / Yet few so much admir'd / Ripen'd for Heav'n by Grace divine / Like Autumn Fruit he fell / Reader think not to live so long / But seek to live as well.* The fondly remembered minister died in 1778, aged 88. EG

**Loughwood Meeting House, Devon** • Baptist chapel • *1653* • *Given by Devon and Cornwall Baptist Corporation Ltd, 1969*

# Baroque bedroom

*Above* · William Herbert, 1st Marquess of Powis, in a portrait of around 1690 by François de Troy (1645–1730) at Powis Castle, Powys (NT 1180915).

To enter the State Bedroom at Powis Castle is to be enveloped in Baroque opulence. Dark chocolate grained panelling sets off glittering gilded ornament: a richly carved cornice and frieze of swirling foliage, garlands and swags, draped between four gilded lions' masks, and a heavily scrolled cartouche holding aloft the royal cypher 'CR', most likely in celebration of the Restoration of the Monarchy in 1660 (see page 72).

This room was created by William Herbert, 1st Marquess of Powis (*c*.1626–96), following his inheritance of Powis in 1667. Inspired by royal palaces, his state apartment was a progression of rooms giving increasingly privileged access: the Grand Staircase, Blue Drawing Room (saloon), Library (ante room), Oak Drawing Room (withdrawing room), culminating in the State Bedroom. The latter was reserved for the highest status guests, ideally a monarch. Centred on exclusive access to the area around the state bed itself, its purpose is to host the levee, a practice adopted by English royalty and aristocracy from the Court of Louis XIV. Taking its name from the French 'lever', meaning 'rising', the levee was a formal gathering centred on the dressing of an important aristocratic or royal person. The alcove, appropriately theatrical as the stage for

this ritual, survives complete with its balustrade and railing. It is unique in the UK.

Herbert employed artists and designers operating under royal patronage to create his state apartment, including Gerard Lanscroon (1655–1737), who painted the ceiling of the Grand Staircase. His son, the 2nd Marquess, continued to enrich the rooms, commissioning Lanscroon to paint the Grand Staircase walls, and the ceilings of the Blue Drawing Room and Library.

Although Herbert is not recorded as hosting royal visitors, in 1684 the 1st Duke of Beaufort, Herbert's brother-in-law, visited in his capacity as Lord President of Wales. The visit was documented by his antiquarian companion Thomas Dineley, who described 'a pleasant Bed-chamber with Alcove wherein his Grace ye Duke of Beaufort lay. The furniture is of Crimson Velvet, fring'd with Gold. Ye ballastars are also richly guilded and diversiy'd'. The furniture described

was replaced around 1725 with the silvered set, possibly by John Belchier, seen today, but the room remains largely unchanged.

The carved balustrade may be the work of William Winde (c.1642–1722), as its design is very similar to the Grand Staircase, which he created c.1675. The bed itself is later, dating from c.1780, and is hung with sumptuous crimson Spitalfields silk cut-velvet of c.1715. The ceiling of the alcove is painted with Neo-classical *trompe l'oeil* coffering, laurel branches and a roundel with a Roman figure. The tapestries depict the story of Antony and Cleopatra.

The transformation of Powis was largely completed while Herbert was in exile in France with King James II (1633–1701), where he died, never returning to enjoy his miniature Baroque palace. EG

**Powis Castle, Powys** · State Bedroom · *1667 and later* · *Given by the 4th Earl of Powis, 1952*

# 'Let Newton be and All was Light'

This unassuming bedroom was the setting for a series of discoveries that have reshaped our understanding of the cosmos.

Woolsthorpe Manor was the birthplace of Sir Isaac Newton (1642–1727), and some of his most ingenious ideas were realised here while exiled from Trinity College, Cambridge, during two outbreaks of the plague between 1665 and 1667. Drawings (some modern recreations) and historic etchings on the walls, said to be in Newton's hand, hint at his mind's workings. William Stukeley, friend and biographer of Newton, wrote that 'the walls, & ceilings were full of drawings, which he had made with charcole. There were birds, beasts, men, ships, plants, mathematical figures, circles, & triangles'.

Limewashed walls glow as golden beams of sunlight pierce the gloom from the south and east. This is the room that inspired one of Newton's greatest experiments. In it he proved, with the use of two prisms and a hole that he is said to have carved in his window shutter, that clear white light is composed of seven visible colours – the spectrum seen in a rainbow.

*Right* · Sir Isaac Newton in a portrait of 1712 by Sir James Thornhill (1675–1734) in the collection at Woolsthorpe Manor in Lincolnshire (NT 427536).

Prior to Newton's experiment, it was believed that light only took colour from materials it passed through. The discovery is immortalised in Alexander Pope's words on Newton's monument in Westminster Abbey: *Nature and Nature's Laws lay hid in Night / God said, Let Newton be and All was Light*. EG

**Woolsthorpe Manor, Lincolnshire** · Newton's Bedroom · *1665–7 · Given through the Royal Society, 1943*

# Carving out a reputation

When the 6th Duke and Duchess of Somerset transformed Petworth into a Baroque palace in the last decade of the 17th century, they used the best craftspeople of the age, many of whom had worked on royal commissions. Among them was the carver Grinling Gibbons (1648–1721), whose miraculously realistic works in limewood, which give the Carved Room its name, still astound today. Horace Walpole, who visited in 1749, wrote of 'birds absolutely feathered, and two antique vases with bas-reliefs as perfect and beautiful as if they were carved by a Grecian master'. He considered the room to contain 'much the finest carving of Gibbins [sic] that ever my eyes beheld', and the consistent quality of every detail on such a large scale is indeed unparalleled.

The principal carvings were arranged in lavish drops and crestings to surround four portraits: those of the Duke (1662–1748) and Duchess (1667–1722) by John Closterman, painted contemporaneously with Gibbons' work, and those purported at the time to be of the Duke's grandparents. There were also seven other portraits and three pier-glasses, all with carved frames, and the whole was set in a room half the size of the existing space, which must have intensified the impression of being 'gloriously flounced all round', as Walpole put it.

It was the 6th Duke and Duchess's great grandson, the 3rd Earl of Egremont (1751–1837), who expanded the room to accommodate great banquets, for which it is still occasionally used. He created something remarkable in its own right, gathering much other 17th-century carving from elsewhere in the house and adding yet more in the same style by his own carver, Jonathan Ritson (1776–1846). This even extended onto the cornice and the ceiling and included frames for Ritson's own portrait and that of Gibbons. The final flourish was achieved by the introduction around 1830 of four landscape paintings by J.M.W. Turner (1775–1851), set below the swagger portraits and at a height best suited for viewing from a seated position at the dining table. The park at Petworth featured in two of the Turners and it could thus be viewed on a summer's evening whether diners were facing the windows or inwards, towards the principal wall. JR

**Petworth, West Sussex** · Carved Room · *1690s and early 19th century · Given by the 3rd Lord Leconfield, 1947*

*Right* · Detail of a lime-wood carving of musical instruments (*c.*1692) by Grinling Gibbons on the east wall of the Carved Room at Petworth.

# With the Bloody Bishop's blessing

Newtown Old Town Hall was purchased and restored in the 1930s with donations from Ferguson's Gang, a group of anonymous benefactors, each with mysterious pseudonyms, who recorded their exploits in their minute book, The Boo. Their donations were delivered to the Trust's London office by disguised gang members, including 'the Nark' (wearing a mask from Harrods) and 'the Bloody Bishop'. At a visit to the hall in March 1934, The Boo, with an accompanying photograph (below right), records the latter, 'Chaplain 2 Ferguson's Gang, projecting from a window [of the Council Chamber] of the Newtown Old Town Hall' as she solemnly blesses the site. A big tea of waffles and cakes followed.

While this panelled room has variously been called the Banqueting Hall, Courtroom or, by the Gang, 'large arguing room', it is now commonly named the Council Chamber. Bustling Newtown was awarded two parliamentary seats by Queen Elizabeth I (1533–1603). The Town

Hall, built by public subscription in around 1699, held associated dinners and gatherings. By the 18th century, when the room was altered, the village electorate had dwindled and the borough was increasingly controlled by two local families, a representative from each assured election to one of the two seats. In 1832 Newtown was declared a 'rotten borough' and disenfranchised. Stripped of its purpose, the hall became a school, then a house and eventually an ivy-clad ruin. LP

**Newtown Old Town Hall, Isle of Wight** • Banqueting Hall • *c.1699* • *Given by Ferguson's Gang (a group of anonymous benefactors), 1933*

# Makers' marks

Its red brick turrets crisply crenelated, Tattershall Castle's Great Tower rises from the Lincolnshire Fens, a bold statement of power. Ralph, 3rd Baron Cromwell (*c.*1393–1456), began construction of his six-floor tower in the early 1430s, around the time he received the office of Lord Treasurer to King Henry VI (1421–71).

The second-floor great chamber is the castle's most impressive space, its magnificence increased by the long processional corridor approach, with soaring vaulting and heraldic bosses. The fireplace is crenelated, with foliated spandrels and a traceried frieze, set between deep-revealed perpendicular Gothic windows.

However, in 1693 Tattershall was inherited by the Fortescue family, who, living far away and unimpressed with its antiquated medieval architecture, rented it out as a farm. Cromwell's residence now housed cattle, and a dovecote was installed in his former privy chamber in the south-west turret off the great chamber. This astonishing structure has a timber frame, supporting lath and plaster walls that hold 259 nesting boxes, as well as wooden perches. The moulded earthen surface is alive with graffiti and the tool and finger marks of its makers. EG

**Tattershall Castle, Lincolnshire** · Dovecote · *c.1700* · *Bequeathed by Marquess Curzon of Kedleston, 1926*

# 'A Great Number of Usefull Books'

Libraries in the early 18th century remained essentially private spaces, outgrown closets to the owner's bedchamber, and more often than not they were dominated by practical books that enabled wealthy landowners to pursue their interests and to manage their business affairs. Nowhere is this more true than at Dunham Massey, where George Booth, 2nd Earl of Warrington (1675–1758) had been taught the value of books from a young age. When he rebuilt the house in the early 18th century, he equipped it with a dedicated library room. It survives today almost exactly as he knew it, with its floor-to-ceiling shelving filled with books – many of their spines stamped and gilded with his monogram – scientific instruments in contemporary cases and, set above the fireplace like an altarpiece, Grinling Gibbons's first known carved work, his *Crucifixion after Tintoretto*. The Earl amassed some 2,000 volumes during his life and these were appropriately described in the inventory taken following his death as 'A Great Number of Usefull Books'. JR

**Dunham Massey, Cheshire** · Library · *c.1725* · *Bequeathed by the 10th Earl of Stamford, 1976*

# Making an entrance

The year is 1789 and William Willoughby Cole (1736–1803), descendant of Plantation colonist Sir William Cole (*c.*1576–1653), has been elevated to Earl of Enniskillen.

Visitors to his recently completed house, Florence Court, approach along warmly lamplit colonnades that terminate in small pavilions. The central block of the house, built by John Cole I (1709–67) during the 1750s–60s, is of seven bays and richly ornamented. Heavy quoins and keystones, architraves and pediments throw shadows across its façade. The skyline is enriched with balustrading and the whole elevation is beautifully symmetrical.

On entering, the hall, staircase and landing flow together with a sense of movement. They constitute a kind of outside-in wedding cake orchestrated in plasterwork – from the solid Doric, through the lively Rococo of the acanthus pendant cornice and foliated panels, terminating in the majestic Venetian landing.

Reflecting the bold architecture of the exterior, the doorcase and flanking windows are capped by a heavy Doric entablature and this theme is continued in the sandstone chimney-piece, also pedimented and rusticated with a triglyph frieze. It bears a back plate decorated with anchors, the initials I.F.C. and the date

1588, possibly imported from Devonshire by Sir William Cole in 1607.

East and west light suffuses the space at three levels. The sweep of the cantilevered pine staircase with its yew handrail draws the eye upwards to drink in full-bodied Rococo plasterwork. The polygonal half-landing is fully at the back of the house, in a projecting bay, presenting views both downwards to the black and cream stone hall floor and upwards beneath arches to the finely furnished landing.

This space is articulated in ceiling arches and vaulting but not divided by doors and walls. Thus, the 'Venetian Drawing Room' is essentially a generous landing, lit by the great Venetian window, and crowned by a ceiling alive with swirling foliage and diving birds of prey.

The house suffered a terrible fire in 1955, and the National Trust arranged the restoration of the interiors under the guidance of architect Sir Albert Richardson, who re-opened the archway at the foot of the staircase. A terra-cotta colour scheme proposed by John Fowler was rejected in favour of the current contrasting grey and white, which further emphasises the plaster ornament. EG

**Florence Court, County Fermanagh** · Hall, staircase and landing · *Original architect unknown; restored by Sir Albert Richardson (1880–1964) · c.1755 and 1955 · Given by Viscount Cole, 1954*

Decus Culinæ
NO NOISE NOR STRIFE NOR SWEAR AT ALL
BUT ALL BE DECENT IN THE HALL

# Centuries of song

If the smoke-brown walls of this room could speak, they would tell of centuries of servants' gossip, debate, laughter and song. One of their number, John Wilton (*c.*1691–1751), still watches on. He was a disabled man, given a home by Sir Richard Myddelton (1655–1716) and whose portrait, visible to the left of the fireplace in this photograph, was painted by Thomas Whitmore, probably in 1728/9.

This space was created in 1529 as Chirk Castle's principal hall for dining, and the huge oak plank tables still in situ were made for this hall. By 1631, the room was known as 'the ould hall', having been superseded by a new one across the courtyard, now known as the Cromwell Hall. In 1762, however, in another rearrangement, this once more became a dining hall – now for servants – and its tables, benches and other furnishings returned.

Four carved figures from Chirk's lost 1670s staircase also gaze over proceedings. Two greyhounds, a Turkish and an African figure combine heraldry with a demonstration of the early Myddeltons' global trading success. EG

**Chirk Castle, Wrexham** · Servants' Hall · *1529 and 1762* · *National Land Fund, 1981*

# Artistic differences

The light-hearted embracing of medieval forms by the designers of the mid-18th century is usually categorised as 'Gothick', the concluding 'k' distinguishing it from the sober and scholarly Gothic Revival of the 19th century. Among the earliest examples in Ireland, and one of the most substantial in the whole of the British Isles, is to be found at Castle Ward, overlooking Strangford Lough.

This extraordinary building is a place of two halves, one side of the house entirely Classical and the other Gothick. Its builders, Bernard Ward (1719–81) and his wife, Lady Ann Bligh (1718–89), created a sophisticated architectural whole. The Classical tradition lent gravitas to rooms of formal welcome and business, while entertainment and relaxation took place in ultra-modern Gothick spaces.

Lady Ann's drawing room, now called the Boudoir, is the most extreme of the Gothick rooms at Castle Ward. Gothick detailing extends over the dado, the window shutters and the exquisitely crafted mahogany doors, which are in the form of a pointed arch, but it is the billowing plaster ceiling that dominates. Presumably (very loosely) inspired by medieval church vaulting, it is covered with a web of delicate tracery and foliate patterning. The effect is dizzying and makes almost for a fairground experience, although some commentators have had a less playful response – the poet John Betjeman likened it to 'sitting under a cow's udder'.

If this wondrously dotty conceit was Lady Ann's choice, she did not stay long to enjoy it. Having become exasperated by the constraints of life with Bernard Ward she spent her last 15 years enjoying the pleasures of the fashionable spa town of Bath. JR

**Castle Ward, County Down** · Boudoir · *1760s* · *Given by the Government of Northern Ireland, 1953*

# Playful pagodas

Behind Claydon's façade lie some of the most astonishing interiors in England. They are the work of Luke Lightfoot, who was employed by Ralph, 2nd Earl Verney (1712–91), from 1757. Described as having eyes that 'sparkl'd fire' and 'no small spice of madness in his composition', one can believe both while standing in the rooms he created.

The Chinese Room, a fanciful example of the fashion for chinoiserie, is arguably the greatest of them. The alcove, in the form of a teahouse, its front a frenzy of fretwork and Rococo curls, holds a daybed. Inside, so deep you need to step within to see it, is a tea ceremony scene, carved in high relief, in which two mandarins appear to wave at the viewer in delight. Chinese heads seem to peer around the door jambs while pagodas perch on their frames. Throughout, tiny bells hang down like foliage and delicate flowers climb the pagoda columns; the whole room a scene of theatrical playfulness and extravagance. LP

**Claydon, Buckinghamshire** · Chinese Room · *Luke Lightfoot (c.1722–89) · 1757–69 · Given by the Verney family, 1956*

# Equestrian elegance

In November 1768 Sir Francis Delaval (1727–71) wrote of Seaton Delaval Hall 'I am putting up the stable on a grand plan we saw … when we were in Scotland, with stone divisions of the stalls, which I am sure you will like as they are very agreeable to the rest of the building and look very magnificent at Lord Hopetoun's from whence I have got a plan.'

Although Sir John Vanbrugh (1664–1726) conceived of stables in the East Range, this part of the house was a later addition. Its crisp ashlar, finialled stalls and Venetian window are of unrivalled elegance, although the architect remains unknown. Soaring elliptical arches that articulate the space, in combination with smartly architraved hayrack niches, nod at the interior of the Hagia Sophia, Istanbul's Grand Mosque.

Name plates above each stall connect us with their original occupants, Zephyrus, Hercules, Tartar, Regulus, Peacock, Julius, Chance, Prince, Pilot, Captain, Admiral and Steady. It is said that to celebrate its completion, Sir Francis held a banquet down the main aisle of the stables. EG

**Seaton Delaval Hall, Northumberland** · Stables ·
*After 1768 · Accepted in lieu of inheritance tax, and public appeal, 2009*

# Tripping the light fantastic

Hardly could a room be more suited to a
glittering ball than the Saloon at Saltram: the
soft blue, yellow and white hues of the intricate
ceiling would have become kaleidoscopic to
dancing couples far down below, and the light
from a profusion of candles would have flashed
and sparkled on the cut-glass tassels, festoons
and tiers of the mighty chandeliers. They were
a highly successful Regency addition to what is
otherwise the creation of perhaps the greatest
name in 18th-century design, Robert Adam.
He was at the very height of fashion by the
late 1760s and was brought in by John Parker
(1734/5–88, later Lord Boringdon) and his
wife, the Hon. Theresa Robinson (1744/5–75),
to decorate what was at the time possibly the
largest private room in the county – in the largest
house – and he did so with characteristic and
revolutionary panache.

All the elements of the room were under
Adam's control and all were carefully integrated,
from the Neo-classical plasterwork of the
ceiling with inset roundel paintings by Antonio
Zucchi (1726–95) (see page 100) down to the vast
Axminster carpet, which has lozenges, festoons,
roses and paterae to reflect what is above, and
employs a colour palette of breathtaking variety.
Even the gilt-brass door furniture, with delicate

foliate scrolls and tassel-like keyhole covers, is to Adam's design and is similar to those published in *The Works in Architecture of Robert and James Adam* (1773–8).

Adam collaborated with the finest crafts-people and artists of his day: the suite of seat furniture – intended to be placed against the walls, as it is now – is attributed to Thomas Chippendale (1718–79), the elegant bluejohn and gilt-brass candelabra were produced for the corners of the room by Matthew Boulton (1728–1809), the plasterwork is very likely to be by Joseph Rose (1745–99) and foremost among the paintings displayed on the pale blue silk-damask of the walls is a portrait of Theresa Parker by another titan of the age, Sir Joshua Reynolds (1723–92).

This sumptuous ensemble was indeed used for dancing and John and Theresa's daughter-in-law, Frances Talbot, Countess of Morley (1782–1857), described one such occasion in 1810: the great carpet having been rolled up, chalk to prevent slipping was applied to the bare boards 'after an exquisite design of my own, by a celebrated artist from Plymouth'. The North Devon Band, she continued, 'played the dances all the night', while around the room were 'two rows of seats affording comfortable anchorage for about 200 persons'. JR

**Saltram, Devon** · Saloon · *Robert Adam (1728–92)* · *1768–72 · National Land Fund, 1957*

# Frozen in time

The successful management of any great house depends upon a small army of staff, inside and out. One vital regiment is undoubtedly the gardeners. The gardens at Calke Abbey provide two bountiful gifts, beauty and sustenance. It was expected that fresh produce – fruit, vegetables and flowers – would be available year-round.

The walled gardens at Calke were created in 1773 and are made up of multiple compartments, including small flower and physic gardens (for growing medicinal plants), a large kitchen garden and a slip garden wrapped around the south and west flanks of the complex. At the centre, the glass-domed conservatory, gardeners' rooms and fruit stores were all added in 1777. Ranged along the north side of the flower and physic gardens are the Gardeners' Bothy, stove house, and vinery, along with warm pits for the cultivation of sensitive pineapples, melons, cucumbers and violets.

The Gardeners' Bothy still feels like a working place, with a hotch-potch of tools and pots parked where last laid by a busy gardener on the uneven tile floor. The brick walls are busy with ropes and bow saws, pegs hung with hand tools and coils of hosepipe. A Flymo hover mower rests cheek by jowl with an old wooden seed riddle. One wall is dominated by a large cabinet with drawers for seeds of every variety, from asparagus and aster to radish and rhubarb, via lettuce, melon, marrow and parsley. Another is smothered with prizes awarded, year upon year, to Charles Harpur-Crewe for dahlias, cut flowers and eggs at Ticknall Village Shows in the late 1970s.

The warm sugar-bag blue paint has peeled in areas, dry with age, but the brushstrokes of past gardeners are a vivid reminder that this quiet space was once a place of year-round activity. EG

**Calke Abbey, Derbyshire** · Gardeners' Bothy · *1777* ·
*Given to the Government in lieu of capital transfer tax and transferred to the National Trust, 1985*

FLOWER SEEDS
CABBAGE
CELERY
CARROT
CAULIFLOWER
BRUSSELS
PARSNIP
RHUBARB
ONION
RADISH
PARSLEY
STOVE FLOWER SEEDS
HERBS
SAVOY
ASTERS
SALSAFY
SPINACH
BROAD BE

# Total design

The Etruscan Dressing Room at Osterley is arguably the finest example of Robert Adam's 'total
design'. His hand is to be seen in the schemes
for the walls, doors, ceiling, chairs, chimney
piece, chimney board and fire screen; he com-
mented on the taffeta for the curtains and
designed a carpet (though it seems probable
that the latter was, sadly, never executed).

Adam was employed by two brothers at
Osterley, first Francis (1735–63) and later
Robert Child (1739–82) of Child's Bank, working
here from at least 1761 until 1780 both on the
architecture of the house and on the interiors,
particularly those on the principal floor.

Adam designed several Etruscan rooms,
five in total, during the 1770s. Osterley remains
the only one to survive virtually intact. He had
undertaken the grand tour at age 26 and visited
Herculaneum in 1755. He claimed the idea of
applying the colouring, ornament and style –
'the taste' – of ancient Greek and Etruscan vases
to interiors as his own but there were several
likely contemporary inspirations for the style,
from the collection of Sir William Hamilton (1730–
1803), amassed while he lived in Italy and well
known through colour-illustrated books, and the
vases of Josiah Wedgwood (1730–95), to the
published engravings of Giovanni Battista Piranesi
(1720–78), whom Adam had met in Rome.

This room came towards the end of Adam's time working at Osterley and it shows a far greater lightness of touch than his earlier designs, while the cool palette differs from many other spaces in the house. The decoration, created by the figure and ornament painter Pietro Maria Borgnis (c.1742–c.1810), was executed on sheets of paper, pasted to canvas and applied to the walls and ceiling. It lies at the end of a suite of spectacular spaces that Adam designed along the south wing, forming a termination to the state rooms and following the richness of the State Bedroom with its green velvet and extraordinary eight-pillared bed.

By the later 19th century, the space was being used as a schoolroom. George Francis Child-Villiers, 9th Earl of Jersey (1910–98), who gifted Osterley to the National Trust in 1949, remembered having lessons here with his younger sister, Joan, from the age of six, with their Irish governess, Miss Norah Leigh. In oral history recordings he talks of looking out of the schoolroom window at the great wisteria (which survives today) only to be met with the wide-open orange beak of a young cuckoo nesting just below the sill. LP

**Osterley House, Middlesex** · Etruscan Dressing Room · *Robert Adam (1728–92)* · *1761–80* · *Given by the 9th Earl of Jersey, 1949*

*Opposite* · Design drawing for the east wall of the Etruscan Dressing Room by the office of Robert and James Adam, 1775 (Sir John Soane's Museum, London).

# Dainty dairy

There is a delicious coolness to Berrington's Dairy. Tile lined, marble floored, with round-headed niches in which separating bowls sit on stone-topped tables, it is the picture of hygiene, efficiency and domestic organisation.

Dairies had existed at most large houses since medieval times as spaces for storing milk, separating cream, churning butter and making other dairy products. By the later 18th century many became more ornate, often as the work of a dairy was one of the few tasks in which the lady of the house (perhaps with other female guests) might involve herself. Queen Caroline (1683–1737), consort of George II (1683–1760), had one built at Richmond Park in the 1730s, which was described as being amply furnished with utensils of the most beautiful china.

Lancelot 'Capability' Brown (1716–83) designed the park at Berrington while his son-in-law, Henry Holland, designed the new house from 1778, together with three handsome ranges at the back containing the Estate Office, Kitchen, Laundry and Dairy. LP

**Berrington Hall, Herefordshire** · Dairy · *Henry Holland (1745–1806) · 1778–81 · National Land Fund, 1957*

# Taking the plunge

Sir John Soane was a master at handling awkward spaces, and a genius in creating individualistic modern forms using the Classical language of architecture. He exhibited these skills to the full when Philip Yorke, 3rd Earl of Hardwicke (1757–1834), commissioned him to update Wimpole Hall. A domed, apsidal and top-lit drawing room was fitted into the west side of the house and to the east a sliver of a courtyard was utilised to form the Bath House. It is entered dramatically by a pair of round-headed doorways and curving stairs, light flooding in from an oculus in the barrel-vaulted ceiling.

The bath itself, capable of holding over 2,000 gallons of water, has flanking steps to allow the bather an easy descent. Plunge baths were very fashionable in the 18th century, but most were set away from the house to take advantage of a natural source of water, and only a very few, like Wimpole's, had the luxury of piped hot and cold water. JR

**Wimpole Hall, Cambridgeshire** · Bath House ·
*Sir John Soane (1753–1837) · c.1792 · Bequeathed by Mrs E. Bambridge, 1976*

# Crowning glory

A la Ronde, a 16-sided *cottage orné*, was created by cousins Jane and Mary Parminter, and its crowning glory is the Shell Gallery. A narrow staircase passes mirrored Gothic alcoves spilling over with shells and emerges dramatically on a gallery, the central hall visible two storeys below. Over 26,000 shells, pinecones, ceramic, coral, bone and moss fragments, and even a crab, encrust the walls, arranged in panels with feather-collaged birds, embedded in plaster.

A series of grand tours (*c.*1784–91) saw the cousins returning laden with souvenirs – objects of interest and pictures of pastoral landscapes, romantic ruins and Classical architecture – their minds brimming with inspiration. This they poured into their extraordinary creation, crystalising their fascination with the natural world.

The fashion for grottoes and shell rooms found fruition in the mid-18th century blossoming of the Rococo style, crossing the channel with returning grand tourers. Very few examples survive, as they fell out of fashion and are fragile and difficult to care for. EG

**A la Ronde, Devon** · Shell Gallery · *Jane Parminter (1750–1811) and Mary Parminter (1767–1849)* · *1796* · *National Heritage Memorial Fund, bequests from Mr M. Berkeley and Mr A. Brailey and funds from an appeal, 1991*

# Remarkable survivor

Tīpū Sultān (1751–99) was the ruler of the king-dom of Mysuru in Southern India between 1782 and 1799. He adopted the tiger as his emblem. On 4 May 1799, during the Siege of Srirangapatna, Tīpū was killed at the hands of the East India Company.

Following this, the 'Prize Committee' over-saw the customary division of booty. Henrietta Herbert of Powis and her husband Edward Clive, as Governor of Madras, received items including this tent and shipped them to Britain in 1801.

The surviving parts comprise a series of richly decorated cotton chintz panels, likely put together from multiple tents and created during the mid- and late 18th century as a private tent for Tīpū Sultān's use while travelling. It has a billowing big-top roof, and walls printed and painted with voluptuous red blooms on green foliage, all sprouting forth from urns, and bordered with dainty floral motifs and bold geometric patterns. The effect is that of looking out onto an abundant garden from a loggia or veranda. EG

**Powis Castle, Powys** • Tent of Tīpū Sultān • *Cotton chintz and calico, internal bamboo poles and iron shoes • c.1785–99 • NT 1180731 • Purchased with support from the National Heritage Memorial Fund and the Art Fund, 1999*

*Above* • Late 18th-century tiger-head finial from the octagonal throne of Tīpū Sultān (NT 1180713).

# Silent running

Deep beneath the exquisitely executed Neo-classical majesty of Castle Coole's state rooms lies the industrious world of the servant army that kept the wheels of polite society turning.

James Wyatt's 1790 plan shows this room, at the west end of the vaulted basement corridor, flanked by a china store, which became the housekeeper's bedroom, and maidservants' bedrooms.

The housekeeper shared the management of below-stairs operations with the butler, masterminding the smooth-running of the female household, the care of linen, crockery and glassware, the preserving of foodstuffs and management of other consumables.

West-facing, subterranean windows admit light, but no view. The east and north walls are lined with cream- and brown-painted cupboards and drawers. Above these, Chippendale-esque trellised doors provide ventilated storage. The south wall is dominated by a fireplace and cast-iron stove.

Two Tuscan columns support the stone-vaulted ceiling, a barrier between the hot and bustling basement and the refined rooms above.

Today, the basement is quiet, dust has settled. The hearths lie stone-cold. EG

**Castle Coole, County Fermanagh** · Housekeeper's Room · *James Wyatt (1746–1813)* · *1779–1801* · *Ulster Land Fund, 1951*

# Playing to the gallery

The French Revolution and turmoil across continental Europe caused by the subsequent Napoleonic Wars resulted in a flood of important paintings into British collections. The architectural consequence of this was the rapid evolution of picture galleries for the London and country houses of the wealthiest families, the progenitors of the public art gallery. Among the earliest fully fledged examples is that at Attingham Park, designed in 1805 by the Prince Regent's favoured architect, John Nash. His patron was the wildly extravagant Thomas Noel Hill, 2nd Lord Berwick (1770–1832), who on coming of age in 1792 decided upon a protracted visit to Italy. While there he met and patronised contemporary artists, notably Angelica Kauffman (1741–1807), as well as acquiring Old Master paintings, Etruscan vases, sculpture and even a scale model of Mount Vesuvius.

Lord Berwick later admitted to his brother 'not having resolution to abstain from Building and Picture buying', and to accommodate the best of those pictures Nash remodelled the core of the house at Attingham into a vast single space. Out of necessity and for the better viewing of the art, the room was top-lit. Slender, curved cast-iron frames supplied by Shrewsbury ironmaster William Hazledine were used to

create a continuous cove of glazed panels. Such innovative technology evolved to provide the huge spans of glazing needed over railway stations like London's St Pancras, and for glasshouses such as the wonder that is the Palm House at Kew Gardens, also in London.

To add to the glamour and theatricality of the gallery, which was painted then as now in a rich vermilion red with porphyry-effect columns and much gilding, Nash created an extraordinary circular and imperial stair adjacent. The colour scheme is the same and the woodwork, like that of the gallery, has lavish inlays and marquetry, while the domed and fluted upper section gives the conceit of a tented structure. To further add to the puzzlement and delight of those experiencing the stairs for the first time, the doors leading to the upper floor are cleverly concealed. It is as if the purpose is to ascend only in order to immediately descend and thus be returned to enjoy the glories of the Picture Gallery all over again but from an opposite perspective.

All of this came at an enormous cost and Lord Berwick's extravagances led to financial ruin and the sale of the bulk of his magnificent collections in 1827. Fortunately, suitable if slightly less dazzling replacements were acquired by his brother and successor, William Noel-Hill, 3rd Lord Berwick (1773–1842), during his 25 years in Italy as a diplomat. JR

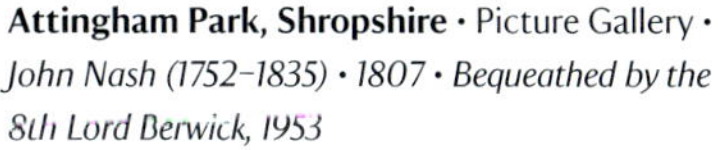

**Attingham Park, Shropshire** · Picture Gallery · *John Nash (1752–1835)* · *1807* · *Bequeathed by the 8th Lord Berwick, 1953*

*Left* · Detail of a French giltwood, marble and ormolu console table of around 1800 in the Picture Gallery, Attingham Park, Shropshire (NT 608145).

# At the anvil altar

Here is a room (when in use) full of heat and noise and smell, where shadows are cast long from the light of the fire; where the metallic rhythm of the smith's hammer is contrasted with that of the water as it churns from the wheel outside; where the industrial age was worshipped, in its way, at the anvil altar; where the contrasts of darkness and light, natural beauty and purpose, man and nature are most acutely felt.

The foundry was owned by several generations of the same family. William Finch (1779–1862), the founder, is first listed as a 'whitesmith' (one who makes and repairs things made of light, cold metals such as tin) but as his family grew and the foundry established itself, so he became a blacksmith (one who works heavier, hot metals). In time, the foundry grew to be one of the most successful manufacturers of edge tools in the South West, producing at its height around 400 tools a day and employing over 20 men. It remained active until 1960, and the Trust continues to keep it in working order and to give demonstrations. LP

**Finch Foundry, Devon** · Forge · *1814* · *Given by North Dartmoor Museums Association, 1994*

## Italian inspiration

William John Bankes (1786–1855) and his architect, Sir Charles Barry, transformed Kingston Lacy in the first half of the 19th century, uniquely merging the relative severity of English 17th-century Classicism with the lavishness of Baroque Rome.

The Loggia was Barry's idea, giving the impression of an open arcade through the use of huge sheets of plate glass and serving as both garden entrance and a landing on the cooly sophisticated Marble Stairs. It was the genius of Bankes, however, to use it also as a family shrine, filling the three niches with statues by Baron Carlo Marochetti (1805–67) of Sir John Bankes (1589–1644), his wife, dubbed 'Brave Dame Mary' (*c.*1598–1661) for her defence of Corfe Castle during the English Civil War, and King Charles I (1600–49), whom they so loyally supported.

William researched every detail meticulously, paying particular attention to Dame Mary, whose 'face, hair and head-dress' were derived from miniatures, while her costume below the waist, not being depicted, was obtained from contemporary French sculpture in the Louvre and at Versailles. JR

**Kingston Lacy, Dorset** · Loggia · *Sir Charles Barry (1795–1860)* · *c.1835–55* · *Bequeathed by Mr H.J.R. Bankes, 1982*

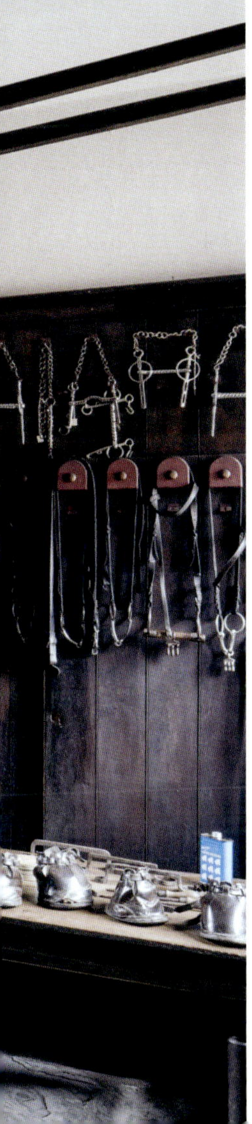

## Trusted steeds, constant friends

Neat's Foot Oil, Brecknell's Saddle Soap, Propert's Boot-Top Powder and ABC Harness Polish stand ready to use. A handsome chimney piece, complete with hot-water boiler, hosted a glowing fire to banish mould from leather and rust from iron and steel.

Stable lads or riders could rest after a long day, once the cleaning of tack and harness was complete, in the well-polished oak armchair and settle. Saddles are neatly stacked, tack and harness hang in ordered ranks, shining bits and stirrups gleam against the dark oak panelling, all clean and ready to use at a moment's notice. Brow-bands, blinkers and harness are emblazoned with the Fairfax and Lucy crests. A neat gallery, accessed by a sturdy folding ladder, provides more storage. The Tack Room was the nerve-centre of the complex of stables and carriage houses at Charlecote Park.

Since Shakespeare was a boy, there have been horses and stables at Charlecote, with coachmen John Thomas and George Banbury, and stable lads Nicholas Thomas and John Thorpe listed on the Lucy family's payroll in the 1570s. The stables, Tack Room and carriage houses are beside the house, indicating the close relationship between the family and their horses. Mary Elizabeth Lucy (1803–90) vividly described the joys and challenges of travelling by carriage, the runaway horses, broken wheels and the ever-present challenge posed by the weather as well as the names of specific horses: trusted steeds and constant friends. The carriages at Charlecote bear witness to the family's extensive travels, with carriages suited to all occasions and distances. All that is missing today are the horses themselves. FB

**Charlecote Park, Warwickshire** · Tack Room ·
*John Gibson (1817–92) · c.1560s and later · Given by Sir Montgomerie Fairfax-Lucy, 4th Bt, 1946*

# Fern frenzy

Diminutive by the standards of its big brother, London's Crystal Palace (1851), the Fernery at Tatton is still remarkable and represents the frenzy for ferns that gripped wealthy mid-19th-century society. Termed 'pteridomania' by the author and naturalist Charles Kingsley, it led to a flurry of fern-collecting expeditions sponsored by wealthy collectors.

In 1859 William, 1st Lord Egerton of Tatton (1806–83), commissioned the renowned Sir Joseph Paxton to create an iron-framed glass-house to display his collection of ferns and tree ferns. Many had been collected in New Zealand and Australia by Egerton's brother, naval captain Charles Randle Egerton (1818–69), some of which still survive here.

Although it is one single space, the plan is L-shaped, with a flattened pyramidal west-end, and a long, narrower eastward leg. The intricate iron frame is held aloft on stone corbels; arch-braced trusses and slender purlins, supporting a great Paxtonian glass roof. The fragile ferns protected beneath this spidery structure are lush and create a tantalising jungle, ripe for exploration. EG

**Tatton Park, Cheshire** • Fernery • *Sir Joseph Paxton (1803–65) • 1859 • Bequeathed by the 4th Lord Egerton of Tatton, 1960*

# Steaming into the sublime

Feeding the Victorian hunger for the sublime beauty of the Lake District landscape and the Romantic poetry of William Wordsworth (1770–1850), the steam yacht *Gondola* was launched in 1860. With an 84-foot (25.6-metre) riveted steel hull, she was designed to transport 200 passengers from the Furness branch line terminus on the shore of Coniston Water, on an elegant water-borne excursion.

Sir James Ramsden, Director of the Furness Railway Company, had travelled to Venice in 1850 and commissioned *Gondola*, inspired by the Venetian *burchielli*, ornate wooden pleasure cruisers with sumptuously upholstered, balconied cabins, bristling with carved columns and spangled with mirrors. The First-class Saloon of *Gondola* was described as 'beautifully finished in walnut wood and cushioned and decorated after the style of the royal carriages of our railways'.

During the mid-20th century, *Gondola* fell into disrepair but was rescued, repaired, refitted and relaunched in 1980, resplendent again with the arms of the 12th Duke of Devonshire, whose predecessor, the 7th Duke, had seen her launched in 1860. EG

**Steam Yacht Gondola, Cumbria** · First-class Saloon · *Jones, Quiggin & Co., Liverpool* · *1859 and 1978–80* · *Acquired, 1978*

# Origin story

James Bateman was an eminent horticulturalist and a committed Christian who believed that Christ's second coming was imminent. The extraordinary garden he created at Biddulph Grange exhibited the plants and cultures of the world that together represented, as he saw it, 'a sign of some great change that is approaching'.

To ensure that those visiting the garden got the point, and did not just waft vapidly around a pretty landscape, he engineered that they should enter via the Geological Gallery. Inset into one long wall were slices through rock strata with associated fossils in an attempt to reconcile the evidence of geology and fossils with the six days of creation described in the Book of Genesis.

The theories of Charles Darwin (1809–82), which became public at around the same time, were to prove far more compelling and the gallery was later abandoned. Its potency historically, and to the story of Biddulph Grange, however, have led to its rescue and meticulous restoration in recent years. JR

**Biddulph Grange Garden, Staffordshire** · Geological Gallery · *James Bateman (1811–97) · 1862 · Purchased with a National Heritage Memorial Fund grant, 2002*

DAY, II

DAY · V

# Cabinet chinois

Waddesdon Manor is a turreted château commanding a hill in the Vale of Aylesbury. It was built as the weekend domain of Baron Ferdinand de Rothschild (1839–98), for high-society house parties and to display part of his magnificent art collection. While the exterior borrows architectural features from Renaissance Loire châteaux, the interior is a Victorian version of an 18th-century Parisian townhouse.

Rothschild was a great collector of *boiseries*, or carved wooden panels, largely from the 1720s–30s. The Green Boudoir is one of the only rooms at Waddesdon where the acquisition of a complete authentic 18th-century French interior dictated the floor plan of the manor, rather than the panelling being adapted to suit the desired layout.

The dark green panels are decorated with a proliferation of cats, monkeys and fantasy Chinese figures and, when in its original home at 21 Rue de Richelieu, Paris, it was known as the 'cabinet chinois' – the boudoir of Suzanne Dodun. A boudoir was a small reception room within a private suite, usually situated between dining room and bedroom, where a lady could withdraw to reflect or to have intimate conversations with her friends. It would have been furnished in much the way it is today – with

seating furniture and a desk at which to write letters. The panelling was described as 'green' when it was sold to Rothschild around 1875 but this particular green probably dates from around 1860.

The decoration is astonishingly rich and includes four over-door panels, which could illustrate the Cycle of Life, with a good helping of Love and Folly: a young woman flanked by monkeys, one holding a swaddled kitten, the other offering her fruit and flowers, while a dove flies from her hand, probably symbolising birth (opposite); a group of cats (and maybe monkeys) playing cards, possibly showing youthful folly; a bewigged monkey taking tea with two companions wearing hats, one of whom smokes a pipe, probably symbolising old age; and a Chinese man in a conical hat, sitting on a pedestal bearing a winged mask of Time, with a warrior paying him homage, evoking the wisdom of old age.

It was to this room that Queen Victoria (1819–1901) withdrew after a lavish lunch in 1890. MJ

**Waddesdon Manor, Buckinghamshire** · Boudoir · *1725–30 and 1875–80* · *Bequeathed by James de Rothschild, 1957*

# Warm welcome

The crackle of the fire in the gleaming black range is the sound that greets you as you step from the bite of an autumn evening into the magical world of Townend.

Iron pots hang from ceiling hooks, while cupboards, shelves and tiny drawers (right) are cleverly worked around a languidly tick-tocking long-case clock – the Downhouse is a riot of intricately worked surfaces. Easily mistaken for 17th-century furniture, this is in fact largely the handiwork of George Browne (1834–1914), who was known to carve dates some two centuries earlier. Meticulously thought out and eminently practical areas for detailed work, such as the little writing desk, are set near to the windows to pour light onto the task in hand.

Invisible at first, the meat loft is hidden above the fireplace. Great slabs of meat were hung here to slowly dry and smoke, wisely preserved against the lean winter months.

This is a delightful case of vernacular terminology – the Downhouse is so-called because it is downhill from the earlier core of the house, the Firehouse. EG

**Townend, Cumbria** · Downhouse · *1880s and earlier* · *National Land Fund, 1948*

# 'A place of reunion and a place of transit'

It took just five years for the paint manufacturer Theodore Mander (1853–1900) to realise that the house he had built at Wightwick was not big enough. Working with his architect, Edward Ould, he almost doubled it in size in 1893. Foremost among the rooms he added was the Great Parlour, a full-height space that took as its primary inspiration the great halls of late medieval and Tudor England, notably those in timber-framed manor houses. Mander was intellectually engaged with the latest theories on architecture and design, attending Oscar Wilde's lecture on 'The House Beautiful' and owning a copy of John Ruskin's *The Seven Lamps of Architecture* (1849). He was also guided by the eminent designer, Charles Eamer Kempe, whose inspiration came from a meticulous understanding of historic ornamentation.

Rooms modelled on the great halls of old were revived with the intention of creating an atmosphere as described by the novelist Henry James (1843–1916): 'Bright, large, and high, richly decorated and freely used, full of "corners" and communications … a place of reunion and a place of transit.' The Great Parlour comprised all the pertinent late medieval features including a screens passage and a huge bay window

flooded with light. A rich decorative scheme was provided by Kempe including stained glass and the gold-highlighted plaster frieze. Beneath the frieze are panels of William Morris's woven wool 'Diagonal Trail' and his 'Acanthus' wallpaper is to be found in the bay. Morris & Co. also provided Georgian Revival seat furniture, with 'Strawberry Thief' and 'Bird' pattern upholstery, which was to sit among genuine antique pieces. All was to be arranged in groups about the room to encourage informal gatherings and the scene was lit by historically inspired electrical fittings by George Jack (1855–1931) for the Morris firm and by W.A.S. Benson & Co. Richness and colour was further enhanced by a profusion of Chinese and Japanese porcelain together with Turkish and Persian rugs, while flat-weave Asian fabrics were used for the upholstery and curtains.

The Great Parlour today is presented much as it was in the 1890s, being a rare example of complete decor from the period. Theodore Mander died in 1900, aged only 47, and it was left to the next generation, Sir Geoffrey Mander (1882–1962) and his scholarly second wife, Rosalie Glynn Grylls (1905–88), together with the National Trust, to add an important overlayer of Pre-Raphaelite works to the house. The Great Parlour contains one of the finest of those: *Love among the Ruins* of 1894 by Edward Burne-Jones (1833–98). JR

**Wightwick Manor, West Midlands** · Great Parlour · *Edward Ould (1852–1909) and Charles Eamer Kempe (1837–1907)* · *1893* · *Given by Sir Geoffrey Mander, 1937*

# Plumb-perfect

Margaret Anderson, the Hon. Mrs Ronald Greville (1863–1942), was a society hostess *par excellence* and 'collector of royalties' who entertained lavishly at her London and country houses. Having acquired Polesden Lacey in 1906 she proceeded to have it completely overhauled by the architects Charles Mewès (1858–1914) and Arthur Davis (1878–1951). They had been responsible for the Ritz Hotel in London and knew the importance of luxurious facilities, so Polesden was equipped with bathrooms the like of which were scarcely to be encountered in another country house at the time. There were nine of them to the 14 principal bedrooms and the most luxurious was in Mrs Greville's private apartments on the south side of the house, which enjoyed sweeping views over the surrounding countryside.

Much use of marble was made in Mrs Greville's bathroom – for the floor, for the tiled walls, to encase the bath and even for the shelf above the radiator. Fittings for the bath and pair of basins, along with the WC, were provided by the firm of Wenham & Waters Limited,

sanitary engineers of nearby Croydon, who were favoured for country house commissions and also provided the 'Millais' water closet for the exclusive use of Royal Academicians and associates in Burlington House, Piccadilly. The basins were equipped with an adaptor to take a shower-head attachment – the height of sophistication in Edwardian Britain – and there was no need to plunge one's hands into soapy water to remove the plug thanks to an invisible system operated by a pull-knob between the taps.

Having readied herself in these technologically advanced and luxurious surroundings, Mrs Greville could sweep downstairs to receive her guests, and as most of them had their own, well-equipped bathrooms there was no excuse for being late – something deemed inexcusable by their redoubtable hostess. JR

**Polesden Lacey, Surrey** · Mrs Greville's Bathroom · *Mewès and Davis · 1910 · Bequeathed by the Hon. Mrs Ronald Greville, DBE, 1942*

CREAMERY BUTTER
MacFarlane Lang's
OVAL
PETIT BEURRE
BISCUITS
JACOB & CO

# Heaven scent

There can be few places that so awaken the senses as Mount Stewart, caught between sea and lough and close to the Gulf Stream. Here Edith, Lady Londonderry (1878–1959), created, shared and wrote about her famous gardens – her descriptions full of colour and fragrance. Her home, too, was filled with vibrant, contrasting colours and considered scents.

During her lifetime the house was decorated with huge bowls of potpourri and jardinières full of flowers. Among her personal papers, alongside the seed packets and catalogues, were recipes for potpourri and her own 'sweet jar' – lists of essences and essential oils, verbena and bergamot, red rose and hyacinth, jasmine and marjoram, and recipes setting out how they should be mixed with spices including nutmeg, cinnamon and cloves. It was in the Potpourri Room, tucked just off the Stone Hall, that she and others would gather, strip, dry, pound, cover and stir the flowers used in the production of Mount Stewart's most famous scent. LP

**Mount Stewart, County Down** · Potpourri Room ·
*1920s · Given by Lady Mairi Bury, 1976*

# Sunlit shelter

There were two typewriters for the use of George Bernard Shaw (1856–1950) at his Ayot St Lawrence residence in Hertfordshire. The first was on the desk of his study and the second was in his 'Retreat' – a small wooden summerhouse tucked away at the end of the garden. Here Shaw could seek refuge from the excessive press and public interest that his status as a world-renowned playwright – a superstar of his time – inevitably entailed. When callers enquired after the author of *Pygmalion* (1913) and other revered works, his housekeeper was able to answer truthfully that he was 'out'. He visited daily in all weathers, the electrical connection allowing for a heater and lighting when required. There was also a telephone for such essential communications as the summons to lunch.

The hut was described by Pathé News in 1946 as 'like the writer, strictly practical with no nonsense about it'. This apparently simple construction did, however, have one hidden sophistication – it was mounted on a turntable and thus able to rotate. Shaw, who promoted the benefits of exercise and exposure to sunshine, would put his shoulder to the doorframe as required to follow the course of the sun. In his *Rhyming Picture Guide to Ayot St Lawrence* of 1950 he summed up this productive and clever little haven: 'In shattering sunlight here's the shelter where I write dramas helter skelter'. JR

**Shaw's Corner, Hertfordshire** · Writing Shed · *1920s* ·
*Given by George Bernard Shaw, 1944*

# Ancient and modern

While the architecture of Castle Drogo harks back to a medieval defensive aesthetic, comfort and functionality were all-important to Home and Colonial Stores' founder Julius Drewe (1856–1931) and his architect, Sir Edwin Lutyens. Elegance, quality and simplicity flow through the whole house, and the downstairs service rooms are no less refined than the upstairs spaces dedicated to decadence and comfort. At Castle Drogo Lutyens successfully blends the ancient image of a castle with the very latest in technological advances; architectural alchemy appropriate to a highly successful entrepreneurial client.

Lutyens could be described as a designer as well as an architect, for his work did not stop at walls and roof. He drew, often at 1:1 scale, the fixtures and fittings for his buildings. For Castle Drogo's service spaces he also designed furniture, and every element, from latch and handrail to tap and tile, was executed with diligent attention to detail.

The basement holds a sequence of spaces, connected by a cool stone corridor culminating in the grand trio of kitchen, scullery and larder. The corridor itself has a massive crypt-like granite vault, the stonework sharp with crisply chamfered ribs. The plan form is cranked, and

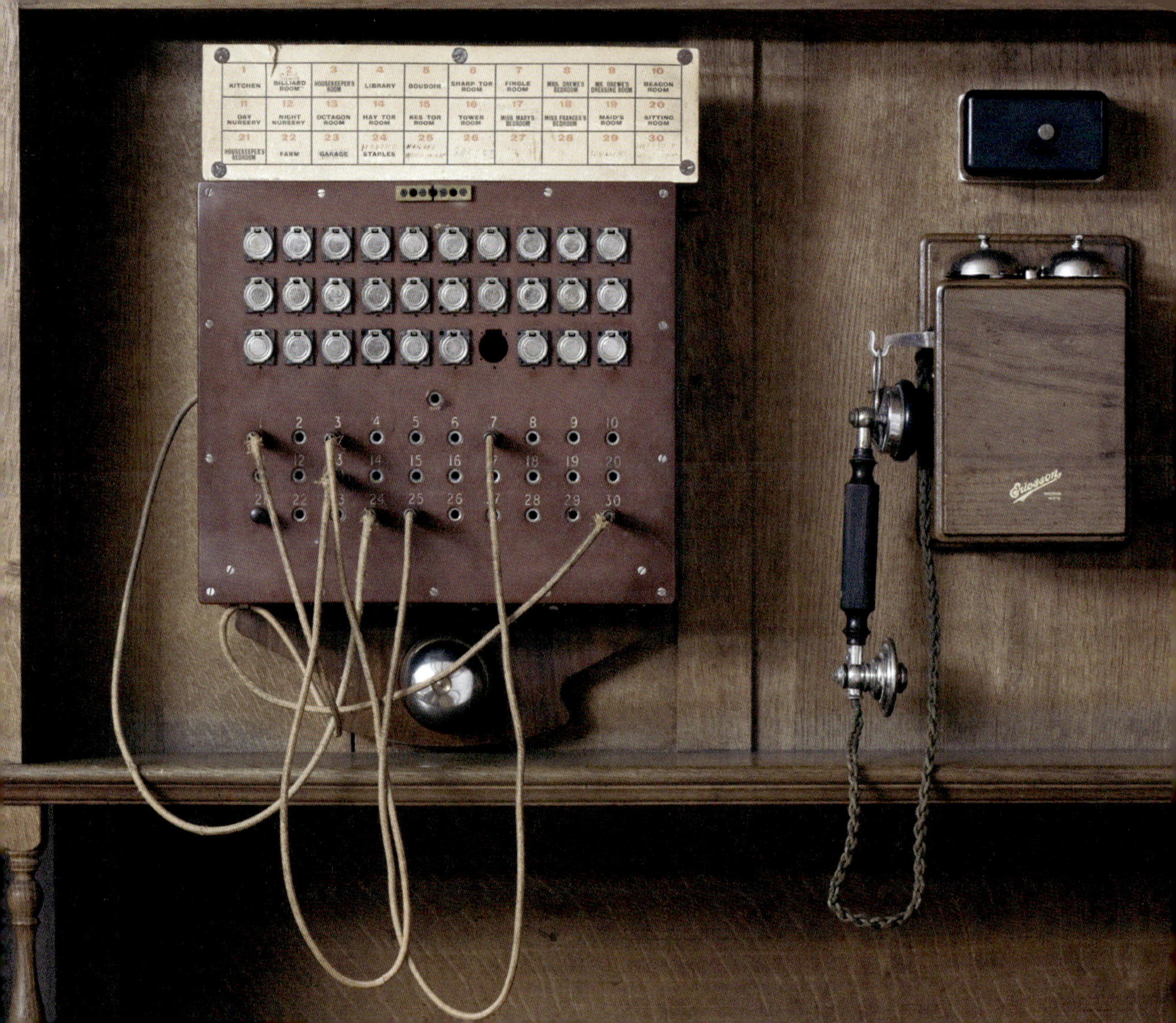

1 KITCHEN
2 BILLIARD ROOM
3 HOUSEKEEPER'S ROOM
4 LIBRARY
5 BOUDOIR
6 SHARP TOR ROOM
7 FINGLE ROOM
8 MRS. DREWE'S BEDROOM
9 MR. DREWE'S DRESSING ROOM
10 BEACON ROOM
11 DAY NURSERY
12 NIGHT NURSERY
13 OCTAGON ROOM
14 HAY TOR ROOM
15 KES TOR ROOM
16 TOWER ROOM
17 MISS MARY'S BEDROOM
18 MISS FRANCES'S BEDROOM
19 MAID'S ROOM
20 SITTING ROOM
21 HOUSEKEEPER'S BEDROOM
22 FARM
23 GARAGE
24 STABLES
25
26
27
28
29
30
Ericsson

at its elbow is the Butler's Pantry, the hub of the household 'machine'. From here, the butler took charge of operations, directing the male staff, briefing them for the day to come. The butler typically set the family's breakfast and led the serving of dinner. His responsibilities also included the care of the most valuable household goods: silver, glass and fine china, as well as stocking the wine cellar.

Entered on its long axis, the Butler's Pantry is pleasingly symmetrical; a solid oak table, pegged, with sturdy bottom rails and turned legs, fills the centre of the room, and oak cupboards, work surfaces and drawers line the pantry walls. An octagonal bay window accommodates a pair of teak sinks, one with three taps (below) – for hot, cold and drinking water, fed from the estate's reservoir.

Supplied with generous quantities of natural light, the Butler's Pantry is also electrically lit, and the entire castle is provided with electricity generated by its own hydroelectric turbine, an innovation first seen four decades earlier at Cragside in Northumberland. To the right of the door is another innovative feature, the castle's telephone exchange (opposite), with 30 labelled extensions, including 'Garage', 'Mr Drewe's Dressing Room' and 'Night Watchman'. In the large lobby area outside the Butler's Pantry stood the household telephone box, the ghost of its panelled walls still visible. EG

**Castle Drogo, Devon** • Butler's Pantry • *Sir Edwin Lutyens (1869–1944) • 1911–30 • Given by Mr A. Drewe, 1974*

# Politics and pleasure

Few domestic spaces in England can have
witnessed such conversations as those held
in the Dining Room at Chartwell, home of
Winston Churchill (1874–1965) and his wife
Clementine (1885–1977) for 40 years. Purchased
in 1922, it was first and foremost a family home
for them and their five children. It was also a
place to entertain (for politics and pleasure)
and the visitors' books reveal the names of not
only friends and family but also politicians,
journalists, scientists, writers and artists.

The house was in need of considerable love,
alteration and extension when purchased by
the Churchills in 1922. They employed the
architect Philip Tilden to undertake the work,
harnessing the steep fall of land towards the
back of the house to create a new Dining Room
below the entrance level, giving directly onto
a terrace lawn, with views to the garden visible
through five large round-headed windows.
While Churchill was very particular about the
furniture, especially the design of the dining
chairs, Clementine chose the Warner's 'Arum
Lily' glazed cotton chintz upholstery and green
curtains, giving the room a delicate freshness
echoing the view beyond. The unstained and
unvarnished oak of the breakfast and dining
tables, commissioned by the Churchills,

supplied by Heals and of plain 17th-century design, and the rush matting enhancing the simple and clean look.

While not large enough to host sizeable weekend gatherings, Chartwell, being less than one hour's drive from London, still hosted many guests and regular house parties. On such occasions lunch was served at 1pm and, in the evening, chilled champagne (usually Pol Roger) at 8pm, dinner at 8.15. Menus, carefully crafted by Clementine, might include lobster salad, pan-seared filet mignon or roast duck, all comple-mented with fresh vegetables and fruit from Chartwell's kitchen garden. Afterwards, once the ladies had retired to the Drawing Room, port, brandy and cigars were consumed.

At other times, when only the family was at home, far simpler fare was served, such as whiting with its tail in its mouth and no sauce, roast chicken, lamb cutlets, sirloin beef or grilled fish, followed by plain ice cream and a ripe Stilton. Tea saw the serving of tomato-and-cucumber sandwiches, with a ceramic pot of Gentleman's Relish always present.

On other occasions, the Dining Room was also the setting for family entertainments, charades and amateur performances, the central curtains being used to create an impromptu stage. In later years it was even converted into a cinema where the family, guests and staff regularly watched films on Sunday evenings. LP

**Chartwell, Kent** · Dining Room · *Philip Tilden (1887–1956) · 1924 · Bought by a group of friends of Sir Winston Churchill and given to the National Trust, 1946*

*Left* · The Churchills and guests in the Dining Room at Chartwell, Kent, photographed by Donald Ferguson on 29 August 1927. Clockwise from his empty seat are Winston Churchill, Therese Lessore, Diana Mitford, Eddie Marsh, Frederick Lindemann, Randolph Churchill, Diana Churchill, Clementine Churchill and Walter Sickert.

# Stellar stable

Smallhythe's old barn, a thick thatch bonnet pulled firmly down over its ears, is so unassuming as to be easily missed. However, behind the rackety timber doors lies an unexpected bubble of theatrical magic. Since 1930, the Smallhythe Barn Theatre has played host to a cavalcade of West End glitterati – stars such as Sir John Gielgud, Dame Peggy Ashcroft and Sybil Thorndike.

From 1899 until her death, renowned Shakespearean actress Ellen Terry (1847–1928) made Smallhythe her home. This was where she escaped from the clamour of London theatre-land, often sharing her sanctuary with theatrical friends. Terry's daughter, the theatre director, costume designer and actor Edith 'Edy' Craig, lived next door and in 1928, following her mother's death, set about turning the barn into a theatre to celebrate her mother's life and work, and to perpetuate the tradition of thespian activity in this quiet corner of Kent.

Smallhythe is now a sleepy hamlet but in the Middle Ages it was a busy port where boatbuilding flourished, supplanted by agriculture as the River Rother silted up. The barn dates from the late 17th century and is heftily built around a rough-hewn oak aisled frame, with weather-boarding, wattle and daub walls, and a reed thatch roof above.

Barn Theatre
E T

The stage sits adjacent to the former threshing floor, and the knees of the audience rub against a timber-panelled grain-barrier. The wings and backstage area are tucked into former feed-bays, and tiny dressing rooms huddle in 19th-century lean-to cattle housing.

This thrilling space delivers a feast for the senses. When in use, the air is thick with a heady combination of long-dried thatch and ancient corn-dust, together with the whiff of greasepaint and the perfume of a closely packed crowd, perched on the edges of their not entirely comfortable seats. Those chairs, each furnished with two cushions against numbness, tell a story. From its original foundation, the Smallhythe Barn Theatre has relied on patronage. Supporters who have paid £1 to sponsor a small rush-seated chair have their names etched in poker-work on each one. Today, one can still sit on the gift of Sir Paul McCartney or Dame Joanna Lumley, elected in 2020 to be only the third in an illustrious line of patrons.

Smallhythe's shrine to Ellen Terry holds hundreds of her finely annotated scripts, and myriad shimmering, silken gowns from her most stellar performances. Terry was iridescent in gold as Guinevere, designed by Edward Burne-Jones in 1895, and as Lady Macbeth cloaked in beetle-wings, as captured by John Singer Sargent (1856–1925) in his 1889 portrait. EG

**Smallhythe Place, Kent** · Barn Theatre · *Late 17th century and 1928–9 · Given by Miss E. Craig, 1939*

*Left* · A painting of 1939 by Clare 'Tony' Atwood (1866–1962) of the interior of the Barn Theatre, with Edith 'Edy' Craig (1869–1947) sitting on the stage, Smallhythe Place, Kent (NT 1118237).

# Bespoke collection

'A room can be filled with innumerable things and yet have a perfect atmosphere of repose, if they are chosen with thought and care so as to form one harmonious background,' wrote Charles Paget Wade in 1945.

Snowshill Manor in the Cotswolds holds over 22,000 such 'things', displayed over 22 rooms and collected over six decades by Charles Paget Wade. The range of objects is varied, from anklets to zithers, as are the names of the rooms they occupy, from Admiral to Zenith. They were collected, curated and cherished by Wade, an architect by training, who inherited land and businesses in the West Indies and purchased Snowshill Manor in 1919. A thin man with long, thick hair 'cut like a sponge', and dark eyes, in later life framed by round tortoiseshell glasses, Wade was often to be seen wearing knee-breeches, ribbed woollen socks and a dark bow tie. When Queen Mary (1867–1953) visited in 1937, it is said she thought that, among the interesting collection of curiosities at Snowshill, Mr Wade himself was the finest!

At the top of the house, in the largest room, once used as a granary and called the Great Garret, can be found the Hundred Wheels. Here Wade gathered many of the objects he had collected relating to transport. They include a collection of twelve 'boneshaker' bicycles from the later 1800s, three- and four-wheeled pedal-operated vehicles, a rare sedan chair that can be converted into a brouette (which has wheels at one end and shafts at the other), a working model of a steam fire engine, and a collection of children's prams, some modelled on farm wagons and one on a hansom cab. Around the room he exhibited scale models of wagons from different English counties and, in the middle, rising from the floor, is a model of a post mill with soldiers who performed various movements when the sails turned. LP

**Snowshill Manor, Gloucestershire** · Hundred Wheels · *Charles Paget Wade (1883–1956) · 1932–44 · Given by Mr C.P. Wade, 1951*

# Fairy-tale tower

Here wrote Vita Sackville-West (1892–1962), novelist, poet and prolific correspondent, surrounded by memorabilia of her travels, her lovers and her family home, Knole. Here she displayed her love of colour – the cobalt and cranberry glass, the bronze green of the cabinet she painted, the faded browns of tapestries and the elephant cord of her daybed and, throughout, the joy provided by the careful placing of Persian turquoise.

In summer, with the windows to her Elizabethan tower room open, the air would be filled with the scent of musk and hay, the perfume of rambling roses and great white lilies. Sometimes, as evening descended, the room would be wrapped in a cloud of Cypriot tobacco from her cigarettes.

This was the first part of the property to be made habitable after Sackville-West and her husband, Harold Nicolson (1886–1968), purchased Sissinghurst in 1930 – the turret room library where she had her first night's sleep and first tea with Harold at a little table, which they carried up the winding tower stairs together. LP

**Sissinghurst, Kent** · Tower Writing Room · *1930s and earlier* · *National Land Fund, 1967*

*Above* · Vita Sackville-West photographed with one of her dogs in the Tower Writing Room at Sissinghurst, Kent, by John Gay in 1948 (National Portrait Gallery, London).

# Love and loss

The expression of unrequited love can take many forms. Rex Whistler poured out his longing for Caroline Paget (1913–73), daughter of the 6th Marquess of Anglesey, in a lavishly painted capriccio. The scene draws upon the family's passion for Venice, marrying it with the rugged Eryri landscape, the setting for the Angleseys' home on the Menai Straits.

Tall windows alternating with mirrored wall reveal slices of the mountainous skyline and reflect the mural opposite. The names of Charles and Marjory Anglesey are captured in grisaille overmantels at either end of the room and the ceiling is a painted paper coffered confection.

The principal players in the tragedy lurk in the shadowy arcades at either end of the room. Spectacles, a discarded book and a pug represent Caroline, and Whistler paints himself as a lonely gardener with a broom (left), sweeping up the red rose petals symbolising his broken heart. Poignantly, this was to be his last self-portrait before he was killed in action in Normandy during the Second World War. EG

**Plas Newydd, Anglesey** · Dining Room · *Architect Harry Goodhart-Rendel (1887–1959) · Painted by Rex Whistler (1905–44) · 1936–7 · Given by the 7th Marquess of Anglesey, 1976*

## Design classic

There are three possible entrances into the Studio on the first floor at 2 Willow Road, London – through the Dining Room, as pictured here, through the Living Room, or directly from the spiral staircase. The same three rooms can be divided by folding panels, as they usually were in winter, or combined into one, as they usually were for parties. This is indicative of the flexible spaces that Ernő Goldfinger designed here in the 1930s.

Goldfinger, born in Budapest, had met Ursula (1906–91), heir to the Crosse and Blackwell fortune, in Paris in 1931, where he had been studying architecture and she art. They moved to London, completing their new home, the central one in a terrace of three, by the summer of 1939. They would raise three children here, with the house at one stage happily accommodating four generations of the same family under one roof.

One wall of the Studio faces Hampstead Heath, its long ribbon window framing a view full of trees and sky, the deep ledges below crowded with found objects – pebbles and pinecones, sculptural wood, tools and carved African figures, glass, ornaments and dried flowers in vases. There is an order both to them and the zoning of the space. The dark grey-green Accotile (thermoplastic) floor tiles are the same here

MAX ERNST

and in the adjoining Dining Room, the wooden
parquet the same on the room's raised platform
and the Living Room beyond. Ingeniously, this
platform contains plan chests; photos taken in
1939 show a polar bear fur rug lying on top. There
is attention to detail in the built-in and door
furniture, the light fittings and switches, nearly
all designed by Ernő. The black laminate-topped
desk, once in his London office, has drawers that
pivot from the table legs and a narrow drawer
concealed within the top itself. The walls, as
throughout the house, display a remarkable
collection of 20th-century art including a photograph of Ursula by Man Ray (1890–1976) and
a 1930 woodcut, *Family Trio*, by Eileen Agar
(1899–1991).

In 1994, 2 Willow Road was the first modern
home to be acquired by the National Trust. LP

**2 Willow Road, London** · Studio · *Ernő Goldfinger
(1902–87) · 1939 · Treasury transfer, with the support of a
special appeal, a grant from the National Heritage Memorial
Fund, and with money from the Headley Trust and a bequest
from Mr H.W. Fletcher, 1994*

*Right* · Press photograph of Ernő Goldfinger from 1968,
when he briefly moved into Balfron Tower, the block of
flats that he designed for the Greater London Council, 'as
a social experiment to help improve his future designs'.

# Liverpudlian launchpad

Music that defined a generation and gave rise to a worldwide mania emerged from this most unassuming of rooms. 20 Forthlin Road was the home of Paul McCartney in the early years of The Beatles. Living here with their musical dad, Jim, both Paul and his brother Mike's creativity was nurtured and supported, allowing them to influence pop culture for generations to come.

20 Forthlin Road is part of the Mather Avenue development of the Liverpool suburb of Allerton. It was built between 1949 and 1952 as part of Liverpool's post-war housing boom in response to the Liverpool Blitz (1940–2). The Mather Avenue development created a house that 'was a pleasure to live in' for the McCartney family.

Cotton-exchange worker Jim was horticulturally minded, lavishing love on the gardens, whereas midwife and community nurse Mary was more interested in decorating their lovely, modern new home, with its fashionable tiled fireplaces and ebony door handles.

After Mary's death in October 1956, the house grew tired, with springs poking through the chairs and flaking bathroom paint. Paul and Mike chipped in with chores, assisted by aunts who rallied round to help. Paul and Mike remember Forthlin as a warm home. It was a

musical home, too – the piano in the room today is a replica of Jim's upright, which Paul still has.

While still at school, Paul was busy writing and teaching himself how to play the trumpet, piano and guitar. At the same time, Mike was honing his skills behind the camera, learning all he could from the books at Allerton library and taking photos of his brother and his mates, little knowing that his early photos would capture the metamorphosis of four ordinary Liverpool lads into global superstars, whose fans would mob the front gate of his home. This attention eventually led the McCartneys to do a 'midnight flit' in 1963, the impact of Beatlemania making life for everyone on Forthlin Road difficult.

New tenants made various changes, so much of what visitors see today in the Parlour is a recreation – one that owes a significant debt to Mike's early photos. National Trust curators looked past the burgeoning stars to the chairs, wallpaper, mirrors and teacups in order to recreate this ordinary room where such extraordinary musical history was made.

*Right* · John Lennon (1940–80) and Paul McCartney (b.1942) writing 'I Saw Her Standing There' in the Parlour at 20 Forthlin Road, Liverpool, in November 1962, photographed by Paul's brother Mike.

*Opposite* · Mike McCartney visiting 20 Forthlin Road in 2023 during the filming of the BBC television series *Hidden Treasures of the National Trust*.

Sanderson wallpapers had originally been chosen by Paul and Mike from roll-ends of three different and competing patterns, making the designer paper more affordable. The final piece in the jigsaw was the stone-effect paper on the fireplace wall, which was returned to its original design in 2023. KT

**20 Forthlin Road, Liverpool** · Parlour · *Sir Lancelot Keay (1883–1974) for the Liverpool Corporation · c.1950 · Purchased, 1995*

# Existential fret

It is easy to walk past 575 Wandsworth Road without a second glance, so modest is the front of this 19th-century terrace house and so busy the road it sits on. However, to be admitted behind its unadorned, white front door into its narrow hallway is to enter another world.

Kenyan-born Khadambi Asalache was a poet, novelist and British civil servant, who had studied architecture, fine art and the philosophy of mathematics. He spent 19 years decorating the interiors of his home with carved fretwork. Starting in the basement Dining Room (see page 203), initially to conceal a damp patch, the adornment spread out across all the rooms much like a beautiful, creeping plant, enveloping the walls and turning the whole house into an unusual and magical artwork.

In the hall and on the stairs and landing, as elsewhere, the fretwork, carved by hand using a pad saw, includes motifs, shapes and images drawn from Asalache's life and interests, particularly Moorish, Ottoman, Indian and African architecture and design, often juxtaposed with figures and animals. LP

**575 Wandsworth Road, London** · Hall, stairs and landing · *Khadambi Asalache (1935–2006)* · *1986–2005* · *Bequeathed by Khadambi Asalache, 2006*

# For the contemplation of freedom

With the Fairhaven Memorial Lodges, designed by Sir Edwin Lutyens (1869–1944) at your back, walk through the long grass of the water meadow, past the Memorial to J.F. Kennedy, away from the traffic of the road to Windsor and beneath the aeroplanes approaching Heathrow; walk along the foot of Cooper's Hill until you see a small, squat, circular building that seems to have risen from the earth and enter the darkness its single entrance seems to hold; here you will find a room of great stillness and tranquillity designed for the contemplation of freedom, its importance and its preservation.

It was at Runnymede in 1215 that Magna Carta (meaning 'great charter') was sealed. Essentially a peace treaty between King John (*c*.1166–1216) and his rebellious subjects, it has come to be viewed as the embodiment and declaration of the rights of protection, fairness and freedom under the law. While no tangible evidence of the event remains and the exact location at which it took place is unknown, Runnymede has become a place where the ideals of justice, democracy, equality and liberty have come to be discussed and celebrated, a place of memorial and commemoration.

ons, or outlawed or exiled, or deprived of his standing in anyway, nor will we proceed wit

2015 marked the 800th anniversary of the sealing of Magna Carta and two new artworks were commissioned both to honour the event and to further explore its meaning and legacy: *The Jurors* by Hew Locke (b.1959) and *Writ in Water* by Mark Wallinger.

Wallinger, winner of the Turner Prize in 2007, together with Studio Octopi, created a circular building made from local, rammed earth. It offers one entrance but two possible routes around a dark curved corridor between an outer wall and inner chamber, both sharp in their construction but rough in the surface of the material. As you edge your way along this windowless passage you come to an opening and a central room open to the elements and full of light is revealed. The wide oculus and the changing sky it frames are reflected in a circular pool of water beneath, its edge inscribed with reversed and inverted lettering only legible when its reflection is viewed in the water beneath. The words revealed are inspired by Clause 39 of Magna Carta:

'No free man shall be seized or imprisoned, or stripped of his rights or possessions, or outlawed or exiled, or deprived of his standing in any way, nor will we proceed with force against him, or send others to do so, except by the lawful judgment of his equals or by the law of the land.' LP

**Runnymede, Surrey** · Writ in Water · *Mark Wallinger (b.1959) and Studio Octopi · 2018 · Funded by the National Lottery through Arts Council England, Art Fund, the Sigrid Rausing Trust, the Henry Moore Foundation and Lord and Lady Lupton*

# Open-and-shut case

As it catches the light on a warm summer's day, the Glasshouse at Woolbeding resembles a giant, glinting, cut jewel as much as a super-sized Victorian terrarium or sculptural flower bud waiting to bloom.

Designed by Heatherwick Studio and conceived as a collaboration between The Woolbeding Charity and the National Trust, this freestanding 'kinetic room' was completed in 2022. Standing 15 metres tall, it takes four minutes for its ten roof sections of glass and steel (created to resemble the sepals of a flower) to unfold, revealing its subtropical contents fully to the sky above and transforming the structure from a pyramidal glasshouse into something more closely resembling a majestic crown.

Approached via the Silk Route Garden, which showcases plants from the ancient trade route between Asia and Europe across 12 different planting zones, the Glasshouse sits within the historic estate of Woolbeding, itself set within what Prime Minister Benjamin Disraeli (1804–81) once described as the 'greenest valley with the prettiest river in the world'. LP

**Woolbeding Gardens, West Sussex** • The Glasshouse
• *Heatherwick Studio* • *2022* • *Commissioned by The
Woolbeding Charity* • *National Land Fund, 1958*

# Layers of history

As Thomas, 2nd Baron Onslow (1679–1740), and Elizabeth, his wife (*c.*1692–1731), waved goodbye to Frederick, Prince of Wales, and his entourage on 27 May 1729, they also bade farewell to the Onslow family's ancestral home, Clandon Park. Within weeks, dismantling began and spades were in the ground to build a grand and ambitious house in the newly fashionable Palladian style in line with Thomas's 'notion of magnificence suited to his rank and fortune'. The Marble Hall stands at the very heart of this rebuilt home; epitomising its status and beauty while communicating complex messages to those who visit. It is shown here before (opposite) and after (right) the fire that devastated the building in 2015.

Neither Thomas nor Elizabeth, who commissioned it, nor their Italian architect, James [Giacomo] Leoni, who designed it, lived to see this remarkable house and entrance hall completed. It was the antiquary George Vertue who, in 1747, had the privilege of describing '… entring into a most noble and elegant Hall 40 foot high adornd with Marbles pillars carvings bass relievos by Rysbracke stuccos painting guildings &c. most rich and Costly'.

It is not only the size and sophisticated architectural framing of the space that have always

made a lasting impression on visitors, but its adornment with sculptural decorative plaster of the greatest skill and artistry by *stuccatori* Giuseppe Artari (d.1769) and Giovanni Bagutti (1681–*c*.1754) complemented by the exquisite detail of the carved marble chimneypieces and overmantels by John Michael Rysbrack (1694–1770).

Scenes of hunting and feasting indicate the use of the Marble Hall as a grand space for dining and signal the generosity of the Onslow family as hosts. But there is also a more subtle

message about a substantial source of their wealth, as orphaned Elizabeth inherited the vast fortune her uncle, Charles Knight, made from the trafficking and enslavement of Africans. According to Onslow family tradition, the white marble busts of men of colour represent their business interests in the Caribbean and the eastern Mediterranean. Unusually, the now destroyed ceiling had as its central theme the Classical myth of the enslavement of Hercules by Omphale, Queen of Lydia.

We recall this Marble Hall with fondness and its damage in the 2015 fire with immense sadness, but once the present scaffolding has come down and the skilled craftspeople conserving it have left, this special room will once more welcome visitors.

Still the heart of Clandon Park, the Marble Hall retains huge visual power and emotional impact. Now the layers of its original construction have been revealed; drawing attention to and celebrating the many unnamed hands who crafted it, from the humble brickmakers to the finest sculptors in the land. SC

**Clandon Park, Surrey** · Marble Hall · *Giacomo Leoni (c.1685–1746)* · *c.1735, 2015 and ongoing* · *Given by the Countess of Iveagh, 1956*

*Opposite* · An architect's impression of the Marble Hall showing visitors experiencing the conserved marble floor, sculpture and plaster, under the new ceiling and skylight.

# Glossary of terms

**Acanthus** · Herbaceous plant with prickly leaves that is often represented in Classical and Classical revival design, for example in the cornice of the Staircase Hall at Florence Court. It was also a favoured motif of William Morris and can be seen in textiles at Standen and wallpaper at Wightwick Manor.

**Aisle truss** · Truss supported by posts set within a room, creating a gap – or aisle – between the posts (sometimes called speres) and the longitudinal walls. It is a feature of important medieval buildings, such as Middle Littleton Tithe Barn, Lower Brockhampton and Rufford Old Hall.

**Alabaster** · Fine-grained white stone used for carving. Alabaster is used to great effect in the chimneypiece of Hardwick Hall's High Great Chamber. Stunning alabaster-work can also be seen in the Marble Hall at Kedleston Hall, which is based on a Roman atrium, with soaring, fluted alabaster columns.

**Andiron** · Horizontal bar, usually made of iron and raised on feet – two at the front and one at the back. Andirons were placed in pairs in a fireplace to hold burning logs above the level of the hearth. Decorative fronts could be added, and there are fine examples in silver at Knole and in polished steel at Blickling Hall.

**Apsidal** · In the form of a semi-circular or polygonal recess, deriving from the apse of a church. The Drawing Room at Wimpole exhibits apsidal forms as does the Dining Room at Kedleston Hall.

**Arcade** · Series of arches supported on columns or piers, often supporting a roof over a covered walkway. When used for decorative purposes close against a wall with no openings, it is

*Right* · A detail of the Renaissance marble and **alabaster** great chimneypiece and **overmantel** in the Ballroom at Knole, Kent.

known as a blind arcade. Kingston Lacy's Loggia, although glazed, is intended to have the appearance of an arcade.

**Arch-brace** · Curved piece of timber providing bracing between the vertical and horizontal parts of a truss or timber wall frame. Arch-braces are often arranged as opposing pairs, creating an arched opening, as seen in medieval and Tudor structures such as Little Moreton Hall, and later adopted in a slender form by iron-frame innovators including Sir Joseph Paxton, who used it in Tatton Park's Fernery.

**Ashlar** · Stone-block finish with straight-cut edges and slim mortar joints. Plastered walls are sometimes painted or scored to mimic ashlar.

**Balustrade** · Row of uprights (or balusters) supporting a handrail or as part of a parapet, etc.

**Baroque** · Classical design style that is characterised by exuberant decoration, curvaceous forms and an air of pomp and grandeur. The Marble Hall at Clandon, in its original form, is an excellent example, as is the Hall at Beningbrough.

**Barrel vault** · Ceiling construction that takes the form of a continuous semi-circular arch. Examples can be seen at Loughwood Meeting House and the long galleries at Lanhydrock and Chastleton.

**Bastion** · Curving or polygonal projection from a wall, usually defensive but sometimes decorative, particularly in the context of a garden, such as that on Nelson's Walk in Stowe Landscape Gardens.

**Battlement** · Fortified parapet to a building, indented (or crenelated) to allow archers to shoot through the openings and shelter behind the solid uprights, as seen on the stair turrets at Chastleton. Also used decoratively internally, such as on the staircase screen at Gawthorpe Hall, the Hall fireplace at Tattershall and the Morning Room fender at Knightshayes Court.

**Bay** · Division of an elevation or interior space as defined by regular vertical features such as

*Left* · Part of the marble **balustrade** on the Upper Marble Staircase at Kingston Lacy, Dorset.

windows on the façade of Florence Court, pilasters in the Saloon at Beningbrough Hall or timber-framed trusses in Middle Littleton Tithe Barn.

**Boss** · Decorative feature at the intersection of structural ribwork in a stone, brick, plaster or timber vault. Examples can be seen in Tattershall Castle's corridor, Chastleton's Great Chamber or The Vyne's Chapel.

**Caldarium** · *See* **Roman baths**

**Cantilever** · Structural element, such as a step or a balcony, supported only at one end. In a cantilevered staircase, each step is set into the wall on the outer side while the inner appears to be unsupported. Spectacular – and apparently gravity-defying – examples can be seen at Attingham Park, The Argory and Llanerchaeron.

**Capriccio** · Architectural fantasy that combines real and imagined elements in pictorial form to create an idealised or witty scene, as in Rex Whistler's murals at Plas Newydd, Mottisfont and Dorneywood.

**Cartouche** · Ornate and sometimes florid frame, often of oval shape and containing heraldry, entwined initials or an inscription. Examples are to be found in the State Bedroom at Powis Castle.

*Right* · The **barrel-vaulted** ceiling of the Long Gallery at Chastleton House, Oxfordshire, built between 1607 and 1612.

**Chevron** · Serrated, zig-zag pattern of decoration typical of Norman doorways and arches, but also seen in earlier Roman designs, for example the mosaic floor of Chedworth Roman Villa's Grand Dining Room.

**Chinoiserie** · Western imitations of Chinese art and design, often in amalgamation with elements from the arts of other South Asian cultures. They are rarely accurately employed and tend to defer to the European stylistic norms of the time, as in the Chinese Room at Claydon and the State Bedroom at Erddig.

**Chippendale** · Style of furniture and interior design of the second half of the 18th century, revived in the 19th and 20th centuries and named after the famous Georgian furniture maker, Thomas Chippendale. Delicate, finely carved detail is a characteristic, as seen in the Housekeeper's Room at Castle Coole and in the genuine Chippendale furniture at Osterley, Saltram, Petworth and Nostell.

**Classical orders** · Doric is the earliest and simplest of the Greek orders, followed by Ionic, which is characterised by rams' horns or volutes, and Corinthian, in which the capitals are decorated with acanthus leaves. In addition to the three principal Greek orders, Tuscan is a simple Roman order and Composite is a combination of Ionic and Corinthian. The orders define a set arrangement of decorative details from top to bottom of a column, as found in ancient

*Above* · The stone-vaulted **Crypt** at Ightham Mote, a medieval moated manor house in Kent.

Greek and Roman architecture and copied by the architects who developed the Neo-classical style, from the late Baroque of Sir John Vanbrugh at Seaton Delaval Hall, through the Palladianism of Robert Adam at Saltram, Osterley and Croome Park.

**Coffered** · Decorated with a recessed polygonal design, often on a ceiling or the underside of a dome, such as in Kedleston Hall's Saloon dome,

*Above* · A view along the **enfilade** from the Tapestry Room at Nostell, West Yorkshire.

and mimicked in paint on the Dining Room ceiling at Plas Newydd.

**Conservatory** · *See* **Glasshouse**

**Corbel** · Projection from a wall in stone, timber or metal to support the structure above it. Corbels support the iron roof frame of the Fernery at Tatton Park and can also be seen in the Servants' Hall at Chirk Castle.

**Cornice** · Projecting uppermost band of a Classical entablature or a projecting horizontal moulding that 'crowns' a structure or marks the junction with a ceiling. Florence Court's Staircase Hall features a Rococo cornice, as do Mottisfont's Whistler Room and Tredegar's Brown Room.

**Cottage orné** · From the French for 'decorated cottage', this term relates to buildings, often on country estates, which were deliberately designed to look rustic and charming. Although they could be residences, as at Blaise Hamlet and A la Ronde, they might primarily be 'eye-catchers', summerhouses or just covered seats.

**Cranked** · Characterised by a pronounced change in angle, for example of a building's plan – as seen in the layout of the servants' quarters at Castle Drogo – or of a structural member in timber or stone, such as the roof timbers in the Great Hall at Cotchele.

**Crenelation** · *See* **Battlement**

**Crypt** · Underground or partly sunken room, usually beneath a church, as at Gibside Chapel. Similar architectural characteristics can also be found in some domestic buildings, for example in the Servants' Corridor at Castle Drogo.

**Dais** · Low platform for a lectern, throne or at the high-status end of a medieval hall, often featuring a canopy above, as in the Great Hall at Chastleton, or as once stood in the Great Hall at Cotehele.

**Dendrochronology** · Tree-ring dating used to

determine the age of construction timber. The analysis of patterns of growth rings, in comparison with known dated timbers, can be used to determine specific dates of felling – and therefore construction – due to the use of green or unseasoned oak. The technique has been used to date construction timber at many National Trust sites, including Cymryd Isaf, Springhill and Alfriston Clergy House.

**Doric** · *See* **Classical orders**

**Enfilade** · Succession of rooms with doors in line with each other. There are examples in many houses, particularly those of the late 17th and 18th centuries, such as Petworth, Osterley, Nostell, Erddig, Belton and Antony.

**Entablature** · Moulded section, including architrave, frieze and cornice, that runs horizontally across the tops of capitals in Classical architecture, often forming the base of a pediment, as at Florence Court.

**Etruscan** · Inspired by the art of the Etruscan civilisation of central Italy, active between the 10th and 1st centuries BCE. Harnessed to powerful effect by Robert Adam at Osterley.

**Festoon** · Draped form of ornament, usually rounded in form and suspended at either end, as can be seen in some of the elements of the great chandeliers in the Saloon at Saltram and in the form of carved fruits and flowers at Petworth and Dyrham Park. Festoons are commonly employed in furnishing fabrics such as curtains.

**Finial** · Upward-pointing decorative element at the top or corner of a structure, such as the staircase at Chastleton, or on the stalls of Seaton Delaval's stables.

**Foliated** · Decorated with or imitating leaf and plant forms, seen in various expressions at Sizergh, Saltram and Wightwick Manor.

**Forge** · Building that includes a hearth for heating metals before they are hammered into shape. 'Forge' can also refer to the hearth itself. *See also* **Foundry**.

**Foundry** · Workshop for casting metal, for example Finch Foundry. *See also* **Forge**.

**Fretwork** · Carved geometrical patterns either pierced through a surface or in relief, as proliferates at 575 Wandsworth Road and can also be seen in the Chapel screen at Cotehele.

**Frieze** · Band of horizontal decoration around a room or a piece of furniture. Hardwick Hall's High Great Chamber has an exceptionally elaborate and substantial frieze. That at East Riddlesden Hall features plaster dragons, and a table in the Boudoir at Belton has a gilded and ebonised Greek Key frieze.

**Frigidarium** · *See* **Roman baths**

*Opposite* · Khadambi Asalache, photographed in 1988 by Gered Mankowitz, in his dining room at 575 Wandsworth Road, London, with its intricately carved wooden **fretwork**.

*Above* · Examples of **grisaille** painted figures, **ionic**
columns and an ornate **cornice** in the **Regency**
Entrance Hall at Attingham Park, Shropshire.

**Garland** · Decorative band of flowers, leaves or other material, often fixed at either end and in between, forming drapes or swags, as can be seen at Christmas in the Great Hall at Cohehele or in Grinling Gibbons's carved overmantel at Sudbury Hall.

**Georgian** · Era of history in Great Britain and Ireland encompassing the reigns of George I to George IV, from 1714 to 1830. Fine examples of the style at National Trust places include the staircase at Florence Court, the Saloon at Saltram, the Cabinet Room at Felbrigg and the Dining Room at Wallington. *See also* **Regency**.

**Glasshouse** · Structure principally consisting of glass and usually framed with timber, iron, steel or aluminium. Glasshouses typically protect prized, sensitive plants, either growing in permanent beds, as in the case of the Fernery at Tatton Park, or for propagation or temporary winter shelter, and can be on a small, domestic scale, as at Mr Straw's House.

**Gothic/Gothick/Gothic Revival** · Gothic is the term used to describe medieval architecture with pointed arches, and described as Early English, Decorated and Perpendicular. Some of this architectural language was revived in the 18th century and the term 'Gothick' was used to describe this somewhat playful interpretation, as seen at Castle Ward, Claydon and Lacock Abbey. Finally, the Victorian era saw a more scholarly exposition of Gothic Revival, as followed by the Pugins at Chirk Castle, G.F. Bodley at Powis Castle and Clumber, and Arthur Blomfield in Tyntesfield's chapel, where a French Gothic style is used.

**Grand tour** · Educative journey undertaken mainly by wealthy British and Irish young adults, such as the Misses Parminter of A la Ronde, and by artists and designers including Robert Adam, who was responsible for interiors at Osterley, Kedleston Hall and Saltram. Its heyday lasted from the late 17th to the early 19th century, and while France and other northern European countries were included, the principal destination was Italy, for the study of its art and architecture, as well as Greece and other Mediterranean lands.

**Grisaille** · Monochrome painting to imitate shallow relief sculpture, as seen in Kedleston Hall's Marble Hall, the Dining Room at Plas Newydd, Wimpole's Chapel and Attingham Park's Entrance Hall.

**Grotesque** · Fantastical, sometimes bizarre and unnatural decoration, often in the form of wall paintings, as in the Cartoon Gallery at Knole, but also found in sculpture and in the decorative arts, such as the tapestries in the Yellow Bedroom at Lyme Park.

**Hypocaust** · System of central heating whereby hot air is conducted through ducts in the floor. Hypocausts are typical of Roman construction and are to be found at Chedworth Roman Villa.

**Imperial stair** · Staircase that commences as a single flight up to the first landing and then splits

into two. Examples can be seen at Attingham Park,
The Vyne, Wallington Hall and Arlington Court.

**Ionic** · *See* **Classical orders**

**Jacobean** · Period in British and Irish history
associated with the reign of King James I and VI,
from 1603 to 1625. Chastleton and the Cartoon
Gallery at Knole date from this time, as does the
south range of Felbrigg Hall.

**Jardinière** · Large holder, most commonly
ceramic, for flowerpots. There are examples
in most National Trust houses including Mount
Stewart and Wightwick Manor. Upton House has
several examples in the finest Sèvres porcelain.

**Knotwork** · Decorative pattern of interweaving
and looping lines favoured by the Romans, as in
the mosaic floor at Chedworth Roman Villa. Also
prominent in Celtic and Celtic revival design, as
seen in garden sculpture at Mount Stewart.

**Lacquer** · Hard and usually shiny coating applied
to wood and metal and made from waxes and
the resin of trees. Examples of Chinese and
Japanese lacquer furniture can be seen at
Petworth, Penrhyn Castle and Ham House.

**Lime ash** · Economical form of flooring in com-
mon use up to the 19th century. It is formed of
the waste lime and ash produced by lime kilns.
Loughwood Meeting House has a floor of lime
ash and it was extensively employed at Little
Moreton Hall.

**Lozenge** · Diamond-shaped form, as seen in the
ceiling and carpet of the Saloon at Saltram and

*Above* · The mosaic floor of the warm room (**tepidarium**),
the wall flues, dividing wall and **hypocaust** pillars of the
hot room (**caldarium**) and the semi-circular hot bath at
Chedworth Roman Villa, Gloucestershire.

the Great Hall plasterwork at Buckland Abbey.

**Marquetry ·** Inlay of thin veneers of different woods or other materials such as ivory and tortoiseshell, to create a decorated surface on a piece of furniture or panelling, such as the eglantine table at Hardwick Hall and a number of the clock cases at Lyme Park. Also sometimes referred to as intarsia.

**Modernist ·** Early 20th-century movement in architecture and other design that is character-ised by experimentation, use of new materials and a break with the past. 2 Willow Road is an instructive example, as is The Homewood.

**Moorish ·** Related to the Moors, a term used historically for people of Berber and Arab origin from North Africa who ruled much of Spain from the 8th century for about 800 years. Moorish design influences can be seen at 575 Wands-worth Road.

**Neo-classical ·** Architectural style employing stylistic elements from Classical Greek and Roman architecture, such as a portico supported on columns, with decoration including swags, urns and sculpture. The Neo-classical style marked an awakening of interest in all antique forms that peaked in the 18th century. Examples include the Hall at Basildon Park, the Drawing Room at Ardress House and the Temple of Piety at Studley Royal.

**Oculus ·** Round or eye-shaped opening, in the case of a window usually in the ceiling or roof of a space as in the Bath House at Wimpole and *Writ in Water* at Runnymede.

**Old Masters ·** Artists of the past or their work (generally predating *c*.1800); collections of paintings typically found in country house collections, as seen in Attingham Park's Picture Gallery for example.

**Orangery ·** *See* **Glasshouse**

**Ottoman ·** Relating to or influenced by the Ottoman Empire, a vast territory centred on modern-day Turkey that dominated south-eastern Europe, western Asia and North Africa from *c*.1300 to 1922. Ottoman influence can be seen at 575 Wandsworth Road.

**Overmantel ·** Decorative continuation of a fireplace on the wall above the fire surround and mantelshelf, as can be seen in Rex Whistler's fictive decoration at Plas Newydd and in plaster-work over a series of Elizabethan fireplaces at Lyme Park.

**Palladian architecture ·** European style derived from the buildings of the Renaissance Venetian architect Andrea Palladio. It is characterised by Classical forms, symmetry and strict proportion, and was fashionable in Britain and Ireland between about 1715 and 1760. Clandon, Basildon Park, the entrance front of Castle Ward and Stourhead are among the many examples to be seen at National Trust places.

**Paterae ·** Ornamental circular or eye-shaped discs used in relief on walls, in stone or plaster, and also carved into furniture. They can be found in abundance in such Classical interiors as the Saloon at Saltram, the Drawing Room at Castle Coole and the Book Room at Wimpole Hall.

**Pediment** · Gable feature, as derived from a Neo-classical temple, and found over doorways, porches and fireplaces. Pediments can be pointed, probably most commonly, as seen in Sizergh's carved entrance hall screen; rounded, as seen over the altar at Belton's Chapel; or finished with scrolls, as in Powis Castle's Grand Staircase and Tredegar's Brown Room.

**Piano nobile** · Italian Renaissance term for a building's principal storey, containing its most important rooms and usually elevated over a lower floor to indicate its status. It is often taller than the other storeys and externally indicated by more elaborate decoration. Examples can be seen at Hardwick Hall, Cliveden, Florence Court and Kingston Lacy.

**Pilaster** · Narrow, projecting section of wall, giving the impression of a column set flush against a wall, or around a rotunda. Examples can be seen in the Cartoon Gallery at Knole and the Saloon at Beningbrough Hall.

**Plantation** · The Plantation of Ireland took place between the 1550s and 1620s, and saw Irish land confiscated by the English Crown and given to English and Scottish families. Towns and villages were established and control of natural resources, including forests, was taken over by the colonists.

*Above* · The Book Room at Wimpole Hall, Cambridgeshire, created by Sir John Soane in 1806, features arches decorated with plasterwork **paterae** by John Papworth.

*Above* · A door in the Saloon at Kedleston Hall, Derbyshire, flanked by two scagliola (imitation marble) **pilasters** with a **pediment** above.

**Porphyry** · Stone with coarse-grained crystals in a fine-grained groundmass, predominantly purple-red but also green, black and grey. Purple is conventionally associated with royalty, and since Roman times porphyry has been prized as a medium for sculpture and decorative elements of buildings. Hinton Ampner has a fine sculpted collection and mock porphyry is employed at Attingham Park.

**Purlin** · Horizontal structural timber spanning between gable ends or structural internal walls, parallel to the wall top and the ridge, supporting the intersecting rafters. Often exposed in medieval roofs, such as at Cymryd Isaf, sometimes chamfered or moulded, as in Cotehele's Great Hall, and rendered in iron at Tatton Park's Fernery.

**Quoin** · Dressed stone at the corner of a wall or façade, sometimes alternating between long and short (as at Florence Court), serving to create a visually and structurally strong corner, and acting as a decorative device.

**Refectory** · Communal dining room, particularly in a monastic or educational institution. The remains of a refectory are to be found at Fountains Abbey. The term has also become associated with large dining tables of medieval and Tudor style, such as that in the Dining Room at Anglesey Abbey.

**Regency** · Period in British and Irish history roughly equating to the incapacity of King

George III from 1811 to 1820 and the rule of his eldest son as Prince Regent. As a stylistic era it is often extended to cover the period from 1795 to 1837. The Picture Gallery at Attingham Park is Regency, as are the interiors at Ickworth and the Library at Melford Hall.

**Renaissance** · Period in European history during which there was a cultural rebirth of Classical antiquity, manifesting in great palaces such as those of the Medici. In England, the architectural and artistic expression of this revival are visible from *c.*1550 at Knole, Hardwick Hall, Montacute, Newark Park, Lyme Park, The Vyne and Lodge Park.

**Rococo** · Design style originating in France in the early 18th century in which asymmetry, freedom of form, natural motifs and scrolls are key features. It was a playful and animated response to the heaviness of the Baroque. Particularly exuberant examples can be seen at Florence Court and Claydon.

**Roman baths** · Bathing was a key element of Roman culture and numerous complexes were built in Britain during their occupation for public use, notably in the city of Bath. Much rarer were private facilities, as at Chedworth Roman Villa. The bather would proceed from the *tepidarium* (warm room) to the *caldarium* (hot room), which was full of steam, and conclude with the *frigidarium* (cold room), where there was a pool of cold water.

**Royal cypher** · Combination of initials (sometimes entwined) and symbols topped with a crown as the visual identifier of a monarch or other royal individual. Charles II's cypher is prominent in Powis Castle's State Bedroom and Queen Victoria's is cast into the post box at Tintagel's Old Post Office.

**Rusticated** · Approach found in Classical architecture, where stonework is carved and patterned to appear more rugged and strong. Sir John Vanbrugh employs it to great effect at Seaton Delaval Hall.

**Spandrel** · Roughly triangular form between the curve of an arch and the rectangular frame of a feature such as a fireplace or doorway, as seen in fireplaces at Tattershall Castle and Gawthorpe Hall.

**Tepidarium** · *See* **Roman baths**

**Terrarium** · A glass container for growing plants in an environment different from the natural surroundings.

**Tesserae** · Small stone and ceramic tiles used to form mosaics, such as Chedworth's Grand Dining Room floor.

*Right* · The ruined remains of a **refectory** at Fountains Abbey in North Yorkshire, a Cistercian monastery built between the 12th and 16th centuries and among the last to be dissolved by Henry VIII in November 1539.

**Tracery** · Intersecting decorative stone ribwork
in vaulting or windows, creating geometric and
flowing patterns, for example in the cloister at
Lacock Abbey. Tracery can be seen tucked away
in Lindisfarne Castle's Undercroft, suggesting
the space may formerly have been a chapel.
Tracery features widely in Gothick and Gothic
Revival rooms such as Castle Ward's Boudoir.

**Triglyph** · Ornament on a Neo-classical frieze,
made up of a three-grooved tablet, alternating
with metopes – plain, flat, recessed panels – as
in Florence Court's entrance hall, or metopes
embellished with a roundel, bust or other decoration, as seen in Shugborough's Entrance Hall
and Kedleston Hall's Library.

**Trompe l'oeil** · Translating as 'trick the eye', this
is illusionistic, two-dimensional painting intended
to give the impression of three-dimensional
spaces, structures and forms, such as in the
Dining Room at Plas Newydd, the staircases at
Hanbury Hall, Powis Castle and Petworth and
the Whistler Room at Mottisfont.

*Right*: Detail of the **Rococo overmantel** mirror, carved
in the 1750s, in the Drawing Room at Peckover House,
Cambridgeshire (NT 781528).

*Opposite* · The extraordinary **trompe l'oeil** mural of a
smoking urn in a niche with other objects, painted by Rex
Whistler in a drawing room (later named the Whistler
Room in his honour) at Mottisfont, Hampshire, in 1939.

**Wainscot** · Wooden panelling lining a wall or room, as in the High Great Chamber at Hardwick Hall, the Inlaid Chamber at Sizergh, the Great Hall at Speke Hall and the Long Gallery and other rooms at Little Moreton Hall.

**Wattle and daub** · Material for infilling timber-frame to form solid walls. A mix of lime and earth, reinforced with fibres (horsehair or grasses) is applied as a wet mortar over a weave of pliable sticks around rigid stays. This is finished with plaster or limewash, and occasionally with a more decorative finish such as pargeted (moulded or sculpted) plaster. Examples can be seen at Cymryd Isaf, Little Moreton Hall and Lavenham's Guildhall.

**Weatherboarding** · Overlapping wooden boards, usually horizontal, applied to the exterior of a building to provide weatherproofing. It is a key component of the Barn Theatre at Smallhythe and can be seen on many other, often utilitarian, buildings across the country such as the Great Barn at Avebury and the little garden shed in the kitchen garden at Lindisfarne Castle.

*Compiled by Elizabeth Green,
Lucy Porten and James Rothwell*

*Overleaf*: Detail of the elaborate **wainscot** installed in 1564 in the Great Hall at Speke Hall, Liverpool.

# Index

# Acknowledgements

The authors are grateful to Michelle Ogundehin for writing such a warm and insightful introduction to this book. We thank those colleagues who contributed entries: Frances Bailey (former Senior National Curator), Sophie Chessum (Senior Curator, Clandon Park), Mia Jackson (Senior Curator of Decorative Arts, Waddesdon Manor) and Katie Taylor (Cultural Heritage Curator); and Emma Slocombe (Senior National Curator), whose ideas helped to shape this book in its early stages.

We owe a debt of gratitude to all those whose research, recording and analysis have provided the foundation for this publication, representing decades of accrued knowledge about the architectural history and interiors of the National Trust. The skills and dedication of those who conserve and care for the buildings and collections of the Trust, preserving our heritage for current and future generations, are warmly recognised.

The authors also gratefully acknowledge the many members of National Trust property staff and volunteers, curators and archaeologists who have provided and verified information on the various sites.

The authors have found the process of writing this book together utterly joyous, made all the more so by working with such expert and professional colleagues: Christopher Tinker, the National Trust's Publisher for Curatorial Content, who commissioned this book and oversaw its editing, design and production, for his passion and attention to detail; and David Boulting, Editor in the Cultural Heritage Publishing team, for his generosity of spirit, combined with brilliance and wisdom.

We are grateful to Matthew Young for his wonderful cover design; Anjali Bulley for proofreading the book, Christopher Phipps for his indexing and Richard Deal and Dan Kosta at Dexter Premedia for the origination.

We would also like to thank photographers Leah Band and Dara McGrath for new photography of several of the featured rooms, and the property teams for supporting the shoots.

The authors are indebted to Mike McCartney for kindly allowing the use of his photograph for the entry on Forthlin Road.

The National Trust gratefully acknowledges a generous bequest from the late Mr and Mrs Kenneth Levy that has supported the cost of preparing this book through the Trust's Cultural Heritage Publishing programme.

## THE AUTHORS

**Dr Elizabeth Green** is the National Trust's Senior National Curator for Architectural History and has been a curator at the National Trust since 2002. She is the author of *60 Remarkable Buildings of the National Trust* (National Trust Cultural Heritage Publishing, 2023).

**Lucy Porten** is the Senior National Curator for London and the South East and Cultural and Oral Histories. She has been a National Trust curator, working both regionally and nationally, since 2003. She is the author of the guidebook for Osterley (National Trust, 2018).

**James Rothwell** is a National Curator at the National Trust specialising in decorative arts. He has worked at the National Trust since 1995 and overseen the restoration and transformation of many historic interiors. He is the author of *Silver for Entertaining* (Philip Wilson/National Trust Specialist Publishing, 2016).

**Michelle Ogundehin** is a writer, author, brand consultant and presenter familiar to BBC television viewers as a judge on *Interior Design Masters*. She is the former Editor-in-Chief of *ELLE Decoration UK* and internationally renowned as an authority on interiors, trends, wellbeing and style.

# Picture credits

*Every effort has been made to contact holders of the copyright in illustrations reproduced in this book, and any omissions will be corrected in future editions if the publisher is notified in writing. The publisher would like to thank the following for permission to reproduce works for which they hold the copyright:*

Page 2 © National Trust Images/David Brunetti • 4–5, 53, 62, 63, 64–4, 70, 74, 98–9, 100, 107, 114, 158, 170, 172, 174–5, 197 © National Trust Images/John Hammond • 6, 10, 15 (left), 16–17, 80 (right), 184 (right) © National Trust Images/Megan Taylor • 8 (left) © National Trust • 8 (right) © National Trust/Imelda Winn • 9, 46, 180–1, 183 © Annapurna Mellor • 12, 33, 36, 150–1 © National Trust Images/Chris Lacey • 14 © National Trust Images/Nadia Mackenzie • 15 (right), 18, 20–1, 32, 37, 38, 39, 47, 48, 56–7, 76–7, 78, 79, 84, 85, 90–1, 92, 94, 95, 110–11, 122, 123, 125, 130–1, 146–7, 148, 168–9, 173, 196, 204, 208, 212, 213, 214 © National Trust Images/Andreas von Einsiedel • 19, 206 © National Trust Images/Ian Shaw • 22–3, 24, 96–7, 178, 201 © National Trust Images/Dennis Gilbert • 26, 34, 35, 49, 58, 60, 61, 103, 124, 136, 137, 138–9, 144, 145, 164–5, 193, 195 © National Trust Images/James Dobson • 28, 30–1, 42, 54–5, 71, 82, 83, 112, 113, 128, 129 © National Trust Images/Leah Band • 29 © Luigi Thompson • 40–1 © National Trust Images/James Beck • 43, 186–7, 188, 189 © National Trust Images/Andrew Butler • 44, 45 © National Trust/Mike Henton • 50–1, 52, 160–1

© National Trust Images/Nick Guttridge • 59 © National Trust Images/Ian Blantern • 66, 69 © National Trust Images/John Miller • 67, 132, 133 © National Trust/Elizabeth Green • 68 © National Trust Images/David Sellman • 72 © National Trust Images/Paul Highnam • 75, 80 (left), 115, 135 © National Trust Images/Paul Harris • 81 © National Trust Images/Martin Trelawny • 86–7, 88–9, 120, 121, 152, 153 © National Trust Images/Dara McGrath • 104–5, 126, 127 © National Trust Images/John Millar • 106 © National Trust Images/Bill Batten • 108 © Sir John Soane's Museum, London • 116–17 © National Trust/View it 360 • 118, 119 © National Trust Images/Erik Pelham • 134 © National Trust Images/Cressida Pemberton-Pigott • 140–1 © Waddesdon Image Library/Chris Lacey • 142 © Waddesdon Image Library • 143 © Waddesdon Image Library/John Bigelow Taylor • 154 © Keystone Press/Alamy • 155 © National Trust Images/Geoffrey Frosh • 156–7, 159, 210–11 © National Trust Images/Chris Davies • 162–3 © National Trust Images • 166 © National Trust Images/Arnhel de Serra • 167 © The Estate of Tony Atwood/Image: National Trust Images • 171 © National Portrait Gallery, London • 176–7 © National Trust Images/James O. Davies • 179 © Trinity Mirror/Mirrorpix/Alamy • 182 © Mike McCartney • 184 (left), 185 © National Trust Images/Robin Forster • 190, 191 © Hufton+Crow • 192 © National Trust Images/Anthony Parkinson • 194 © National Trust Images/Allies and Morrison • 198–9 © National Trust Images/Peter Greenway

• 200 National Trust Images/Rob Matheson • 203 © Gered Mankowitz/Iconic Images • 209 © National Trust Images/Robert Thrift

*Front cover, clockwise from top left:* Seed drawers, Gardeners' Bothy, Calke Abbey © National Trust Images/Surface View • Saloon ceiling, Saltram © National Trust Images/John Hammond • Stained-glass in the front door at Mr Straw's House © National Trust Images/Chris Lacey • Cartouche, State Bedroom, Powis Castle © National Trust Images/Paul Highnam • Stables, Seaton Delaval Hall © National Trust Images/Dennis Gilbert • Etruscan Dressing Room door, Osterley House © National Trust Images/Bill Batten • Front-door detail, 575 Wandsworth Road, London © National Trust Images/Robin Forster • Key detail from the statue of 'Brave Dame Mary', Loggia, Kingston Lacy © National Trust/Christopher Tinker • *Back cover, clockwise from top left:* Telephone exchange, Butler's Pantry, Castle Drogo © National Trust Images/John Hammond • Saloon chandelier, Saltram © National Trust Images/John Hammond • Servants' bells, Dunham Massey © National Trust Images/John Hammond • *Shield of Achilles*, Dining Room, Anglesey Abbey © National Trust Images/Andreas von Einsiedel • Mosaic detail, Grand Dining Room, Chedworth Roman Villa © National Trust Images/Leah Band • Fireplace detail, Marble Hall, Clandon Park © National Trust Images/Chris Lacey

Published in Great Britain by the National Trust, Heelis,
Kemble Drive, Swindon, Wiltshire SN2 2NA

National Trust Cultural Heritage Publishing



Registered charity no. 205846

ISBN 978-0-70-780472-9

A CIP catalogue record for this book is available
from the British Library.

10 9 8 7 6 5 4 3 2 1

Measurements are given in metric form except where
imperial units, such as miles and acres, will be more
familiar to UK readers.

Publisher: Christopher Tinker
Project editor: David Boulting
Proofreader: Anjali Bulley
Indexer: Christopher Phipps
Additional picture research: Susannah Stone
Cover designer: Matthew Young
Page design concept: Peter Dawson,
www.gradedesign.com

Colour origination by Dexter Premedia Ltd, London
Printed in Wales by Gomer Press Ltd
on FSC®-certified paper

Discover the wealth of our collections – great art and
treasures to see and enjoy throughout England, Wales
and Northern Ireland. Visit the National Trust website:
www.nationaltrust.org.uk/art-and-collections
and the National Trust Collections website:
www.nationaltrustcollections.org.uk